Contents

Giving My Father Back His Name

The Fuller Brush Man Meets the Great American Portrait Artist

By Jerry Strauss

Illustrated By
Lucia Yee-Lipitz

Jelstrad Press

Text copyright © 2019 by Jerry Strauss
Illustrations copyright © 2020 by Lucia Yee-Lipitz
Published by Jelstrad Press
JelstradPress@gmail.com
New York, NY, USA

Library of Congress Control Number: 2020925595
ISBN: 978-1-7923-5778-7
10 9 8 7 6 5 4

Printed in the U.S.A.

In memory of my parents, Dewald and Ilse, who survived Nazi Germany, and as refugees, cherished their lives and the freedom they experienced in America.

Preface

Sitting in my office getting ready for the workday at America's greatest encyclopedic art museum, I opened an all-staff meeting notice about an on-site TEDx event. Although an IT guy, Information Technology that is, I love music and art, and my interest in fine arts had grown during my years of employment at the museum. We were opening a new location and leadership had decided to hold a TEDx event to celebrate the opening of the new branch. And one lucky employee would have the opportunity to give a TED talk about the event's theme "The In-Between" in the new museum venue as part of the festivities. The new building had housed an Alice Neel exhibit back in 2000 and it just so happened that my Dad was the subject of one of her iconic paintings.

The coincidence was too much for me. I had a chance to give a talk to the world about my Dad and that painting in the venue where it had last appeared on public view in New York City. Although my public speaking experience was limited, I decided to go for it and wrote the text, created the appropriate slides, practiced a lot, auditioned and was selected to present at the TEDx event.

That TED talk was the experience of a lifetime. It brought me closer to my Dad and inspired me to better understand his life-changing experiences, living through the horrors of Nazi Germany, Dachau, and World War II.

A few years later, my friend Lucia suggested that since my talk had been so well received at the TEDx event, why not turn it into a graphic novel? Fortunately, Lucia happens to be one of the greatest graphic artists this side of the Mississippi, with a creative vision that brings stories to life. So we worked together to retell my Dad's story. Here it is. Enjoy.

Chapter 1: The Discovery

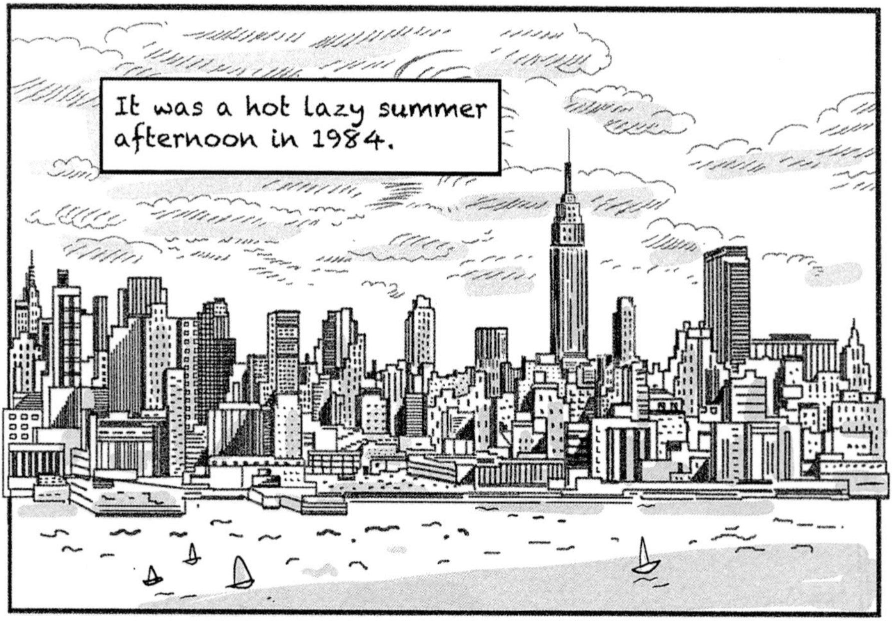
It was a hot lazy summer afternoon in 1984.

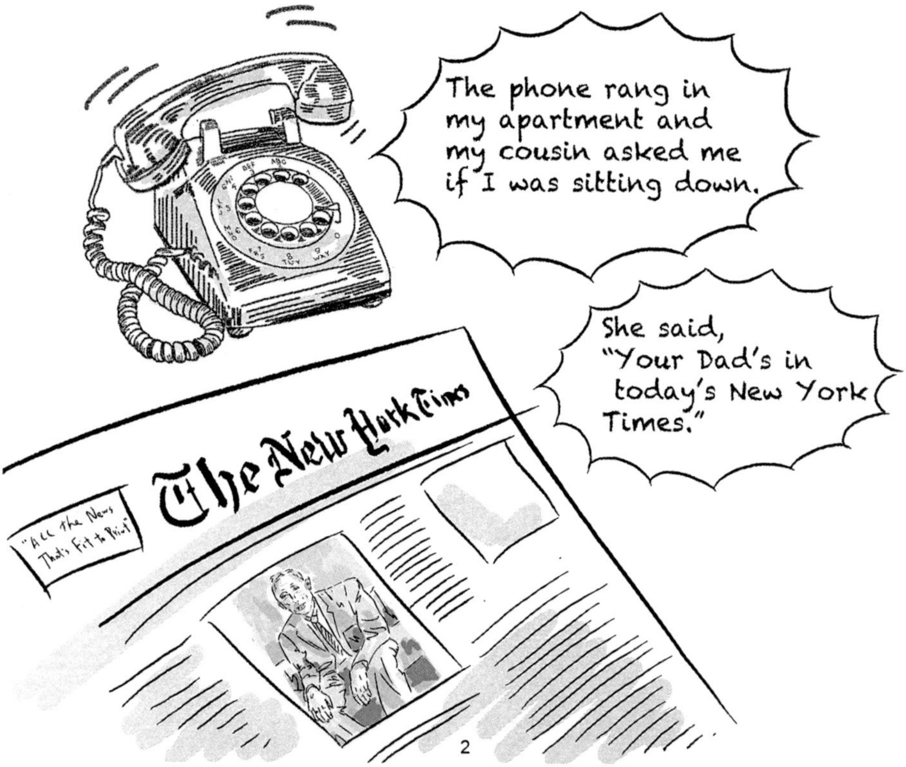
The phone rang in my apartment and my cousin asked me if I was sitting down.
She said, "Your Dad's in today's New York Times."
The New York Times
"All the News That's Fit to Print"

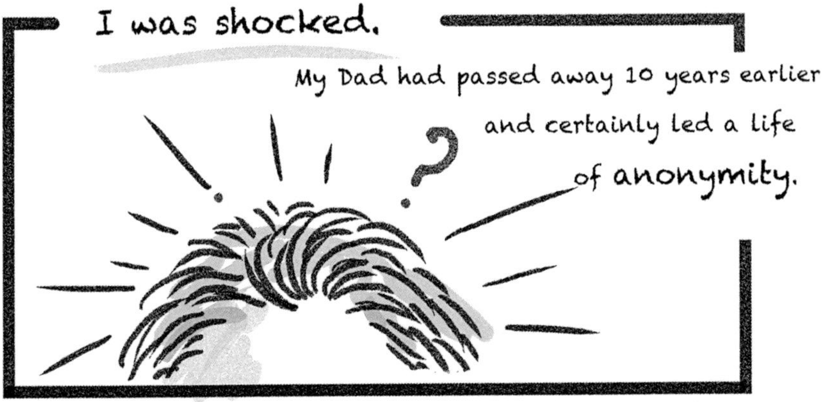
I was shocked.
My Dad had passed away 10 years earlier
and certainly led a life
of anonymity.

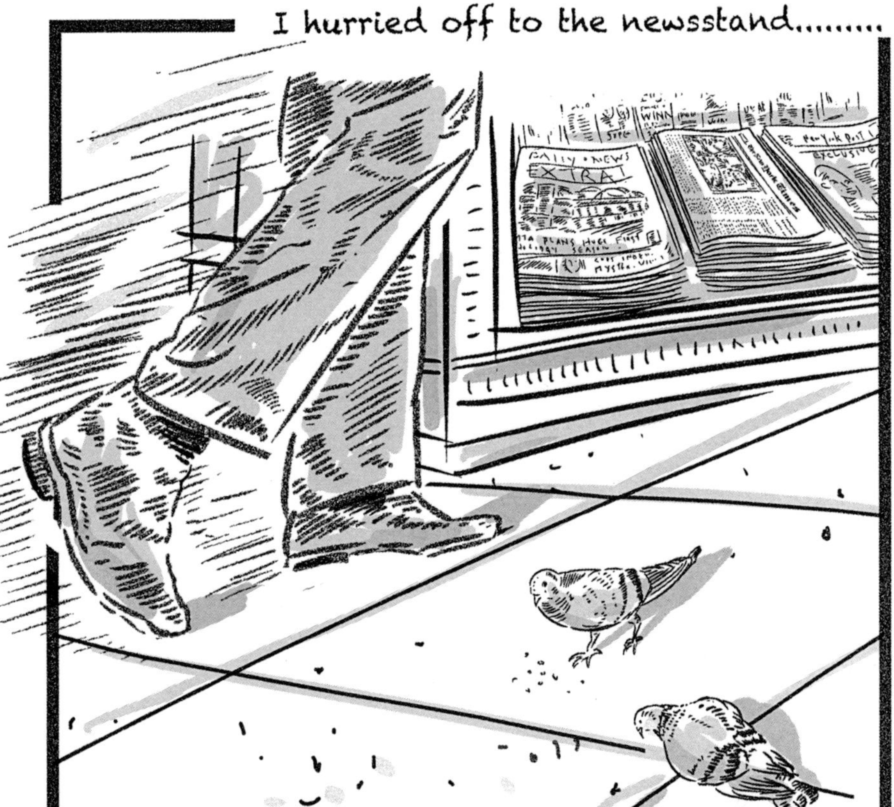
I hurried off to the newsstand.........
DAILY NEWS
EXTRA!

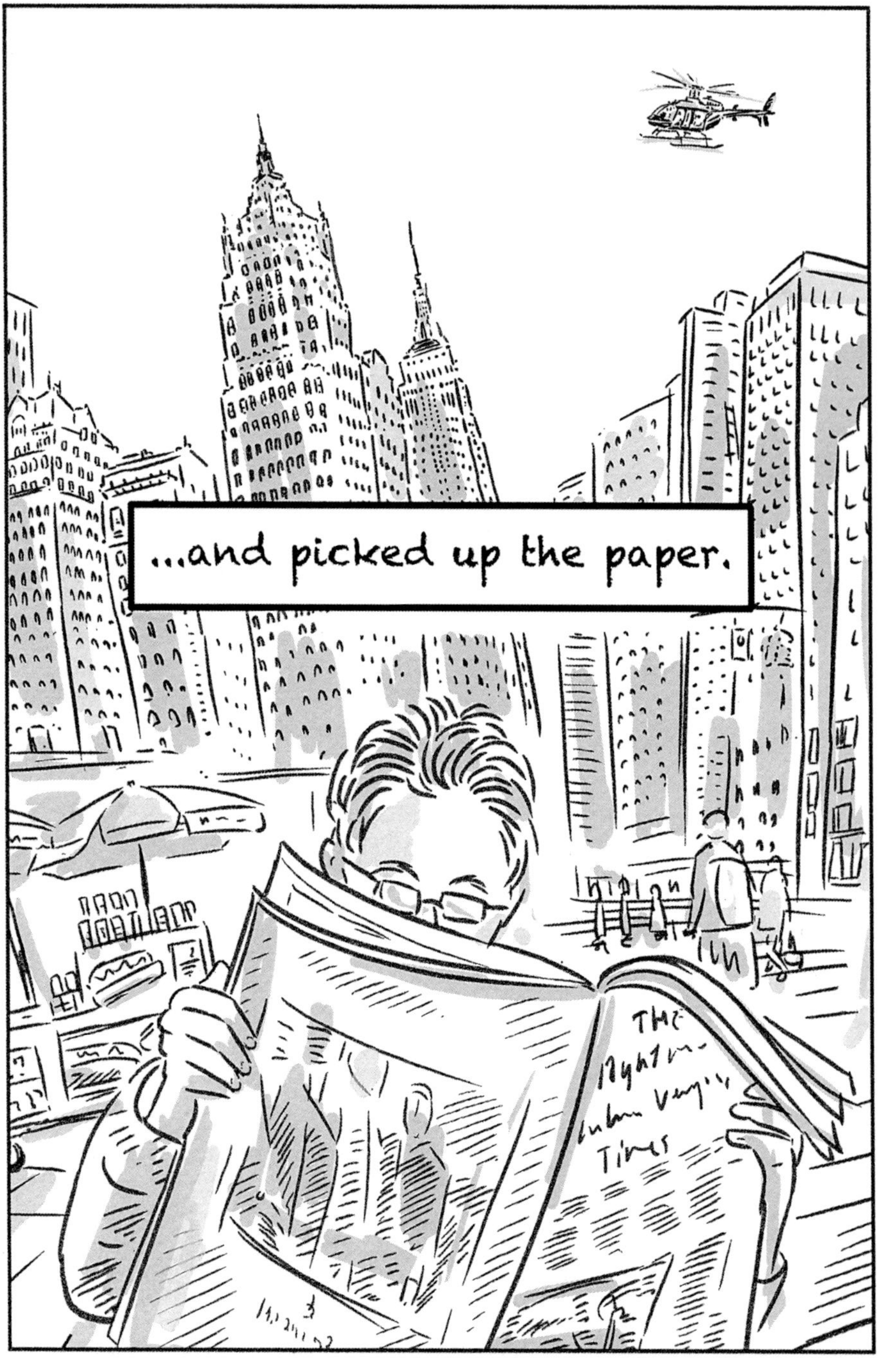
...and picked up the paper.

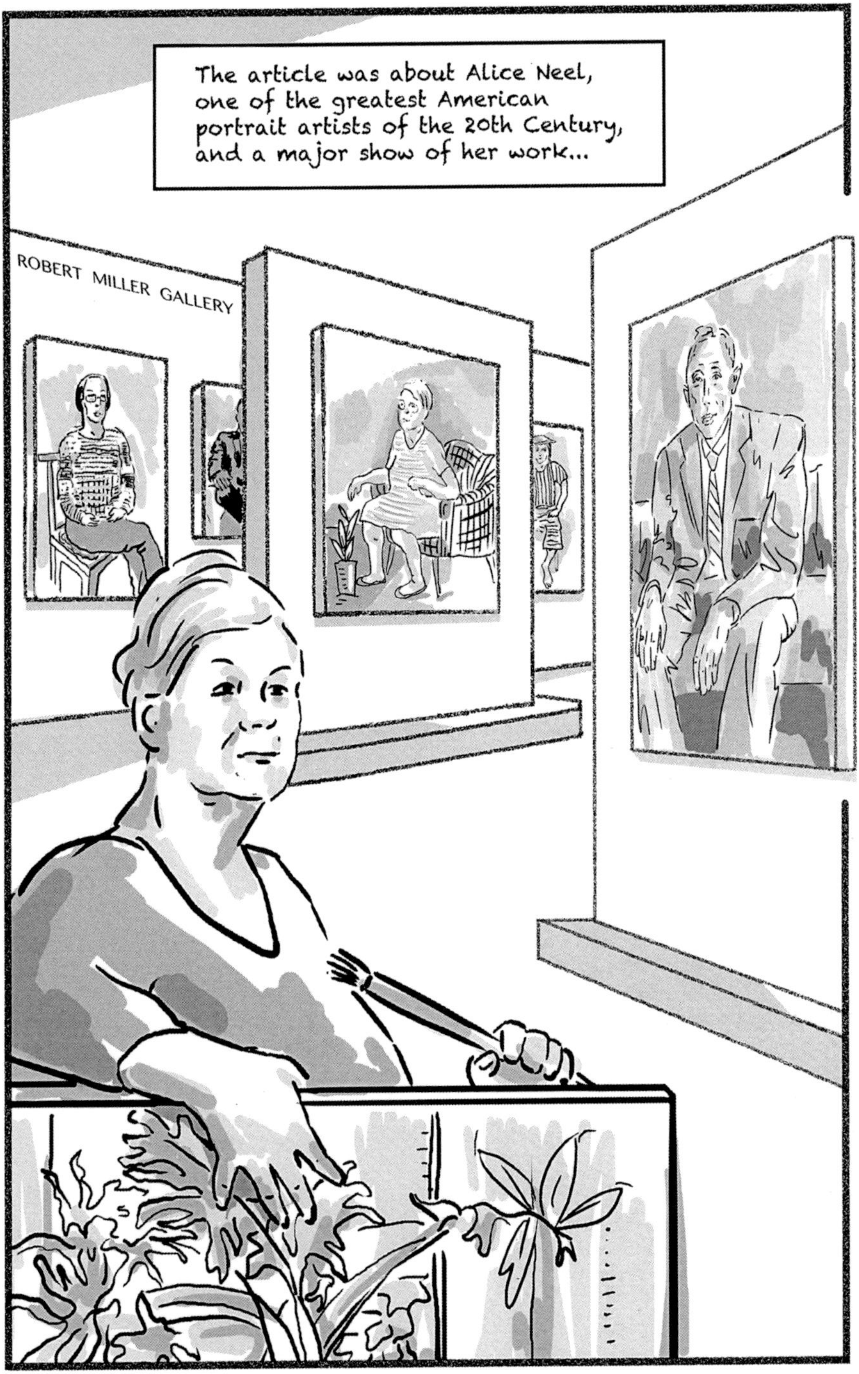
The article was about Alice Neel, one of the greatest American portrait artists of the 20th Century, and a major show of her work...
ROBERT MILLER GALLERY

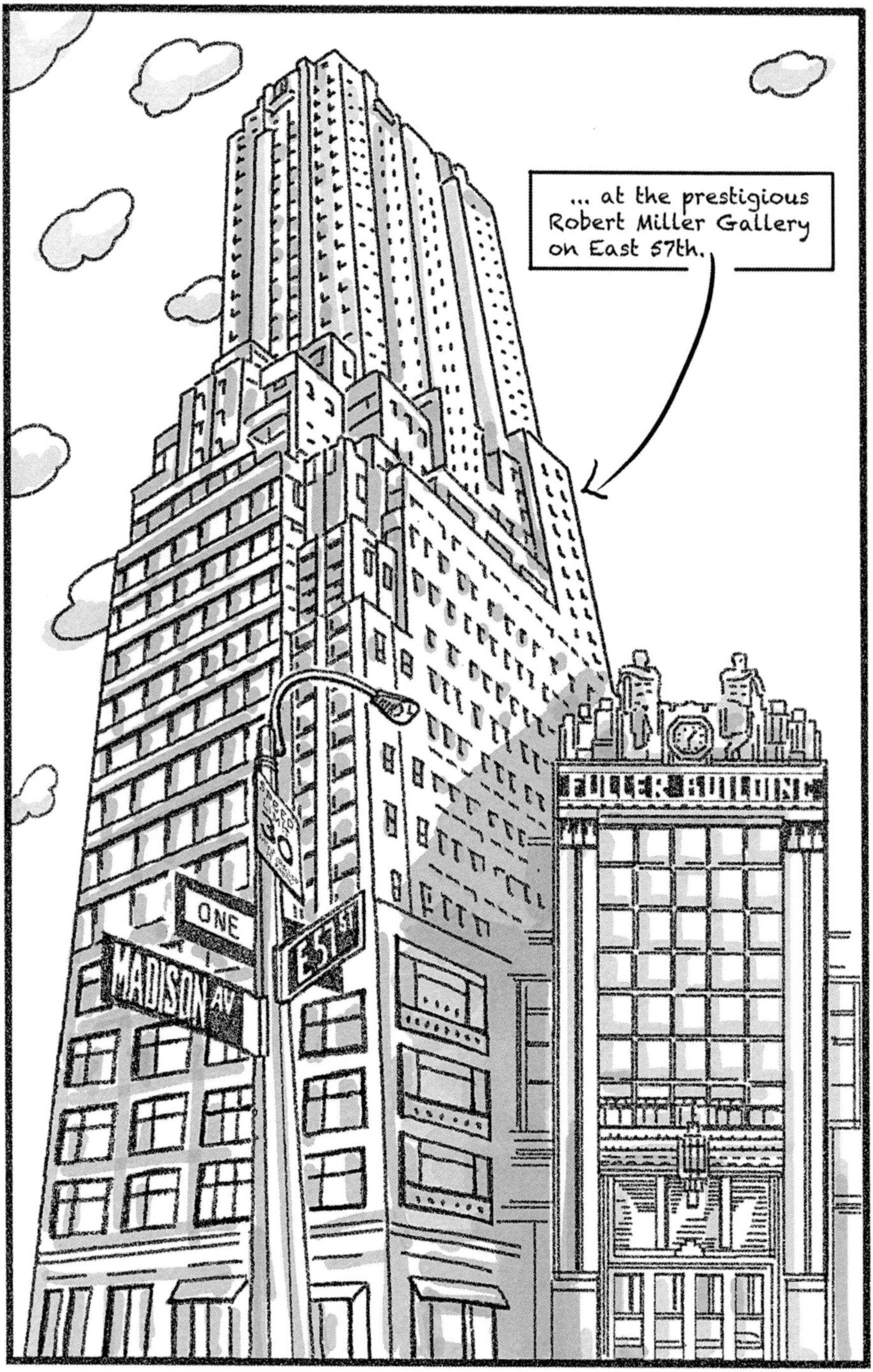
... at the prestigious Robert Miller Gallery on East 57th.
ONE
MADISON AV
E 57 ST
FULLER BUILDING

And the featured painting in the NY Times article was "Fuller Brush Man."

That's my Dad!

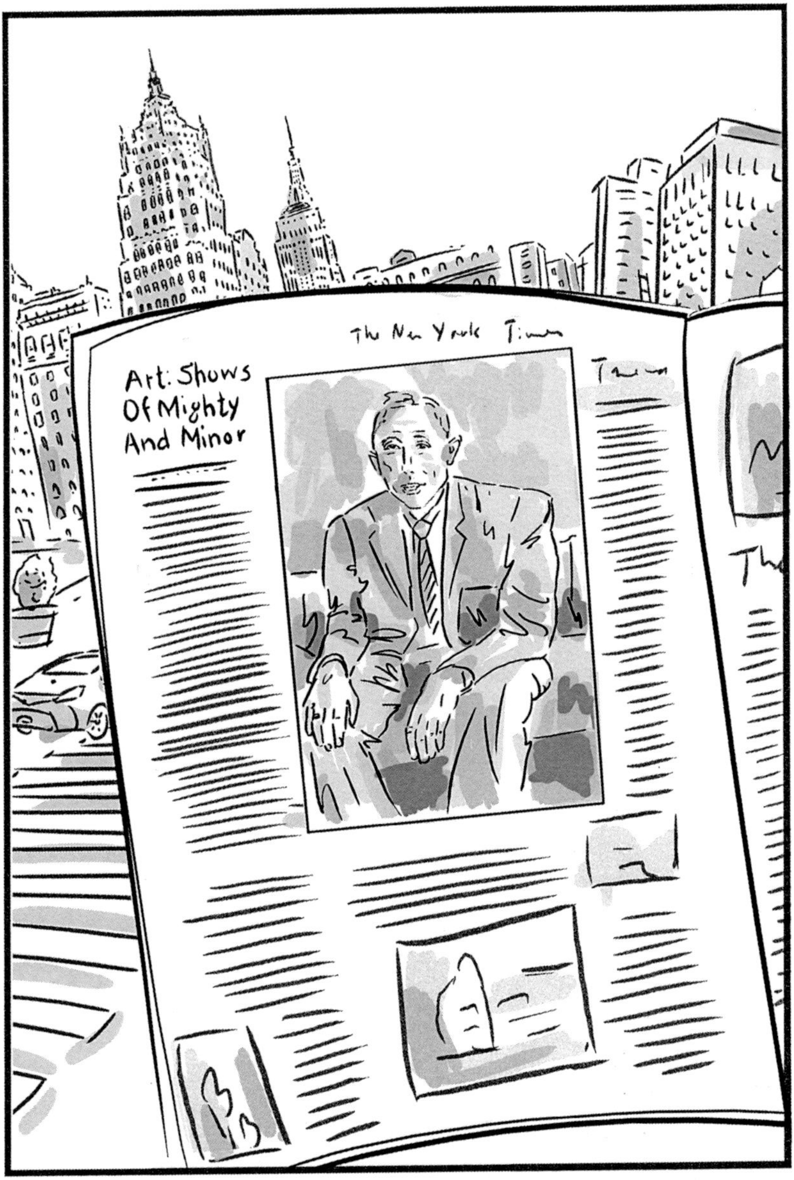
Art: Shows Of Mighty And Minor

Alice had painted it in the '60s.

But my question was, how did this happen?
I didn't know the painting existed.
Then, it all made sense.

Alice Neel was one of his customers!

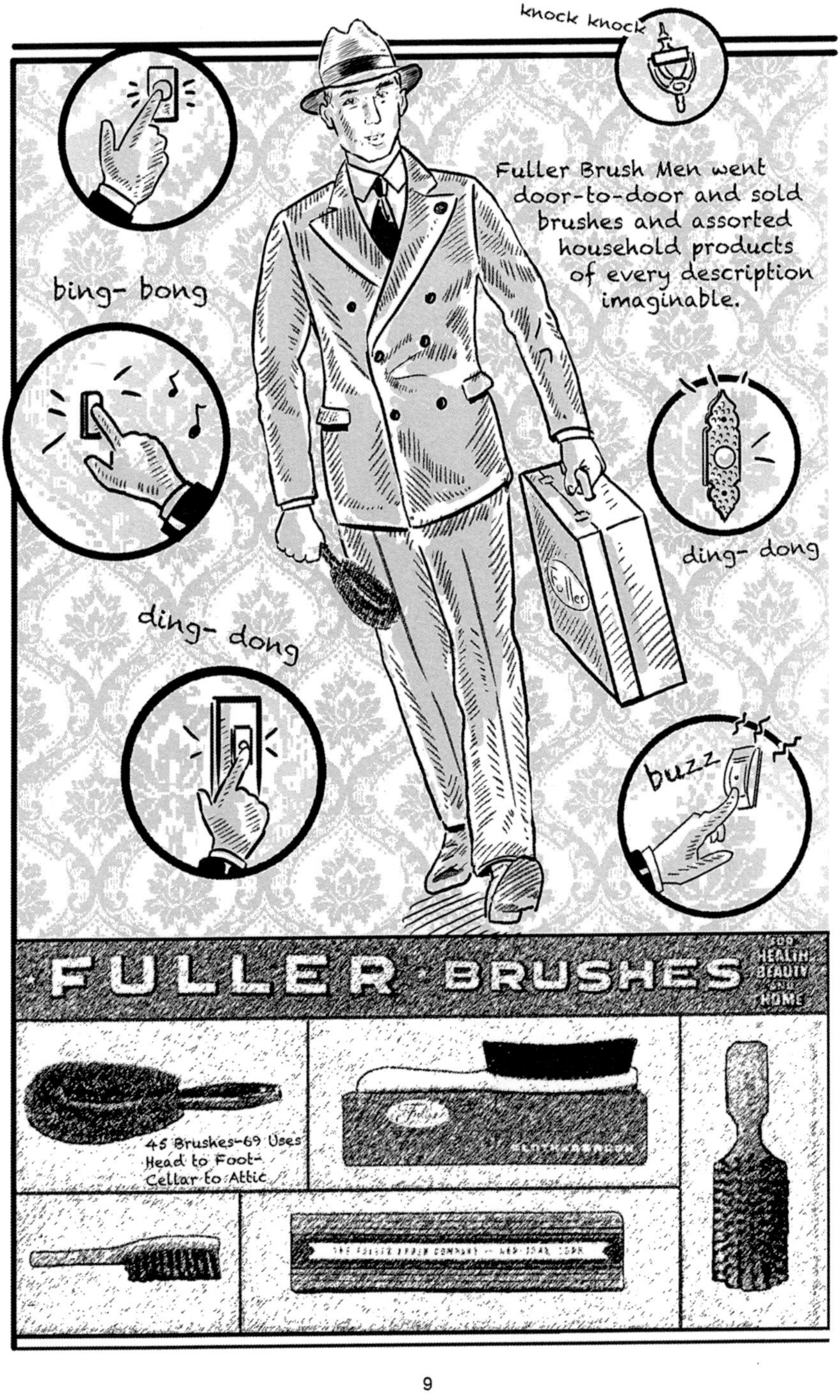
knock knock
Fuller Brush Men went door-to-door and sold brushes and assorted household products of every description imaginable.
bing- bong
ding- dong
ding- dong
buzz
FULLER · BRUSHES
FOR HEALTH, BEAUTY AND HOME
45 Brushes-69 Uses
Head to Foot-
Cellar to Attic

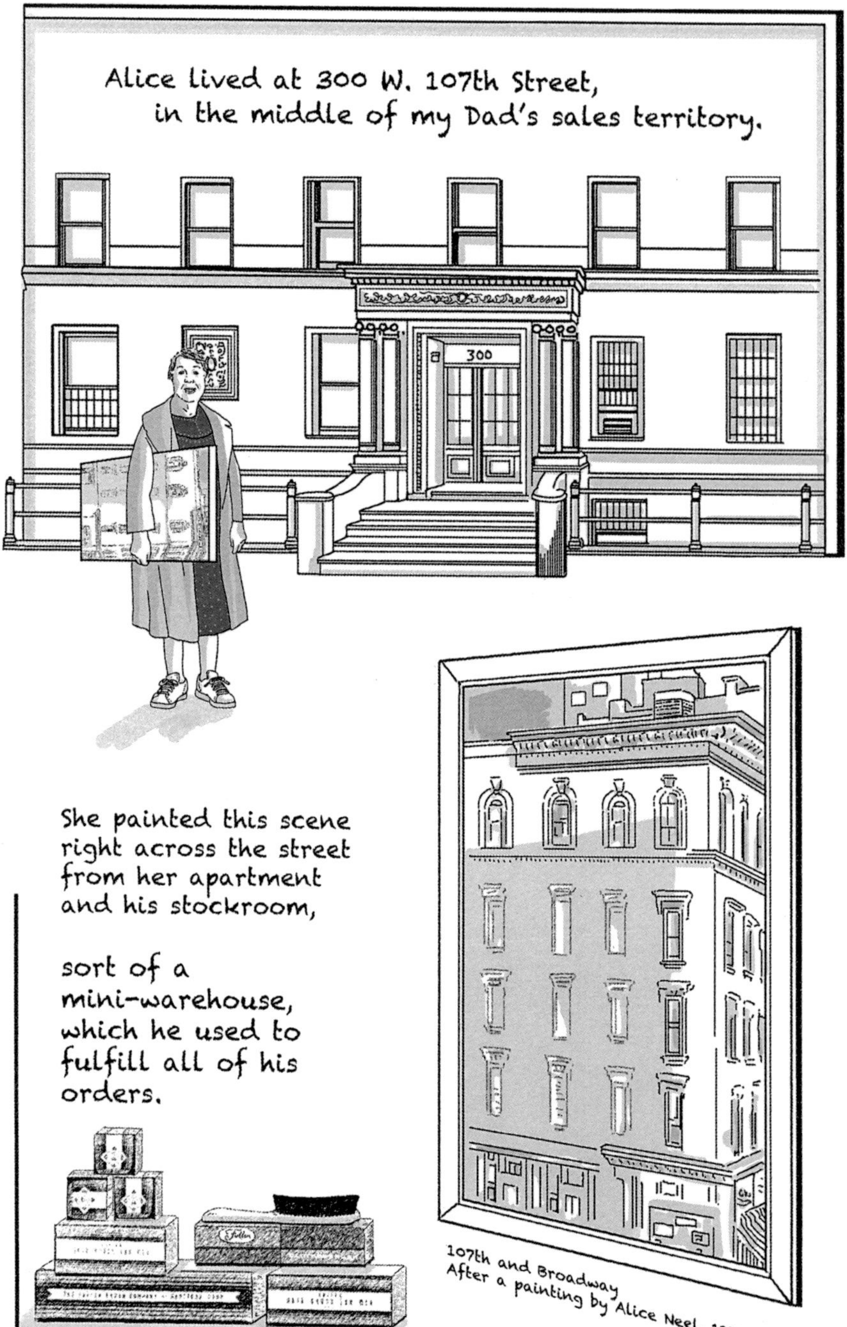
Alice lived at 300 W. 107th Street, in the middle of my Dad's sales territory.
300
She painted this scene right across the street from her apartment and his stockroom,
sort of a mini-warehouse, which he used to fulfill all of his orders.
107th and Broadway
After a painting by Alice Neel, 1976

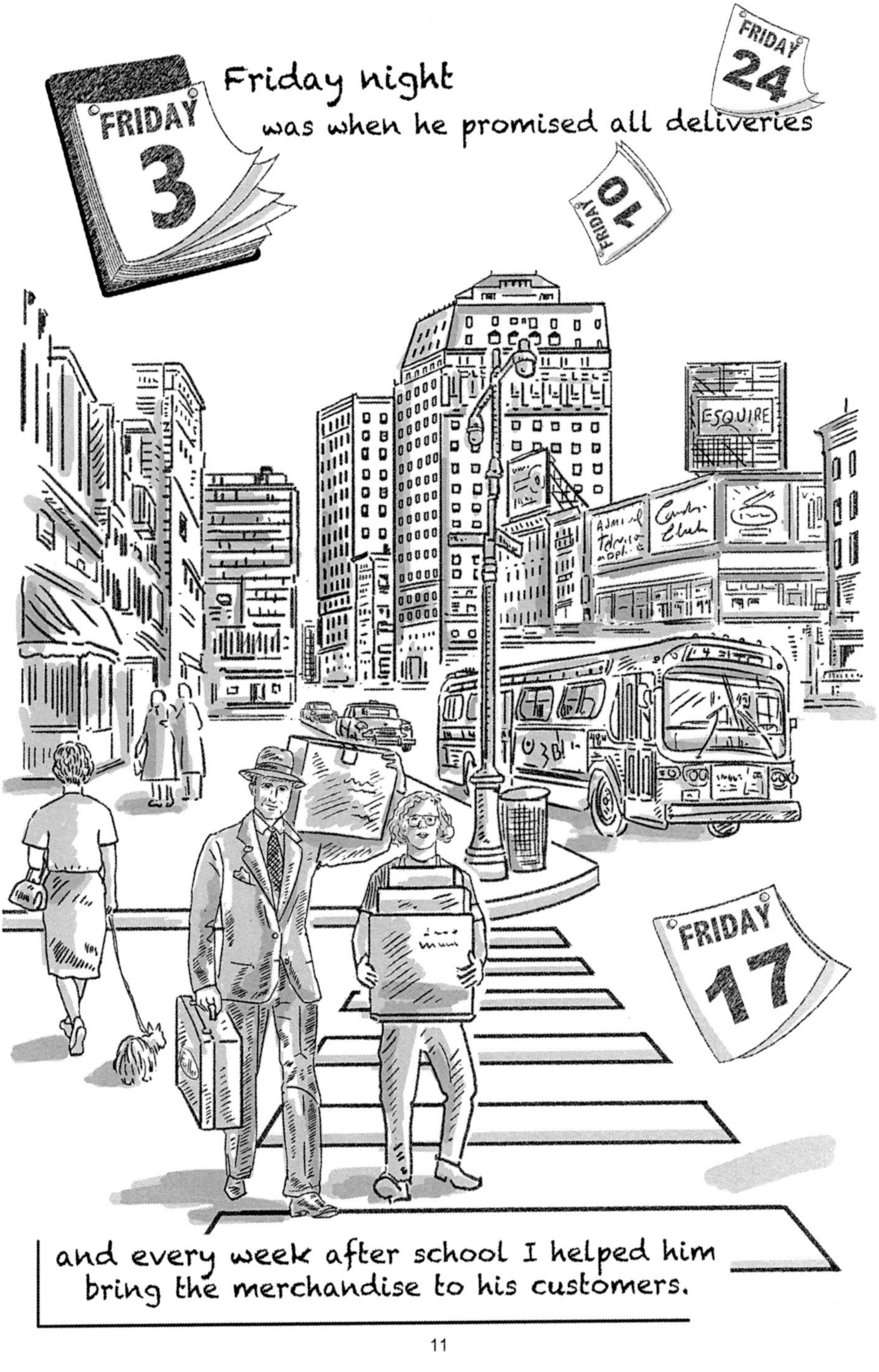
FRIDAY
3
Friday night
was when he promised all deliveries
FRIDAY
24
FRIDAY
10
ESQUIRE
FRIDAY
17
and every week after school I helped him
bring the merchandise to his customers.

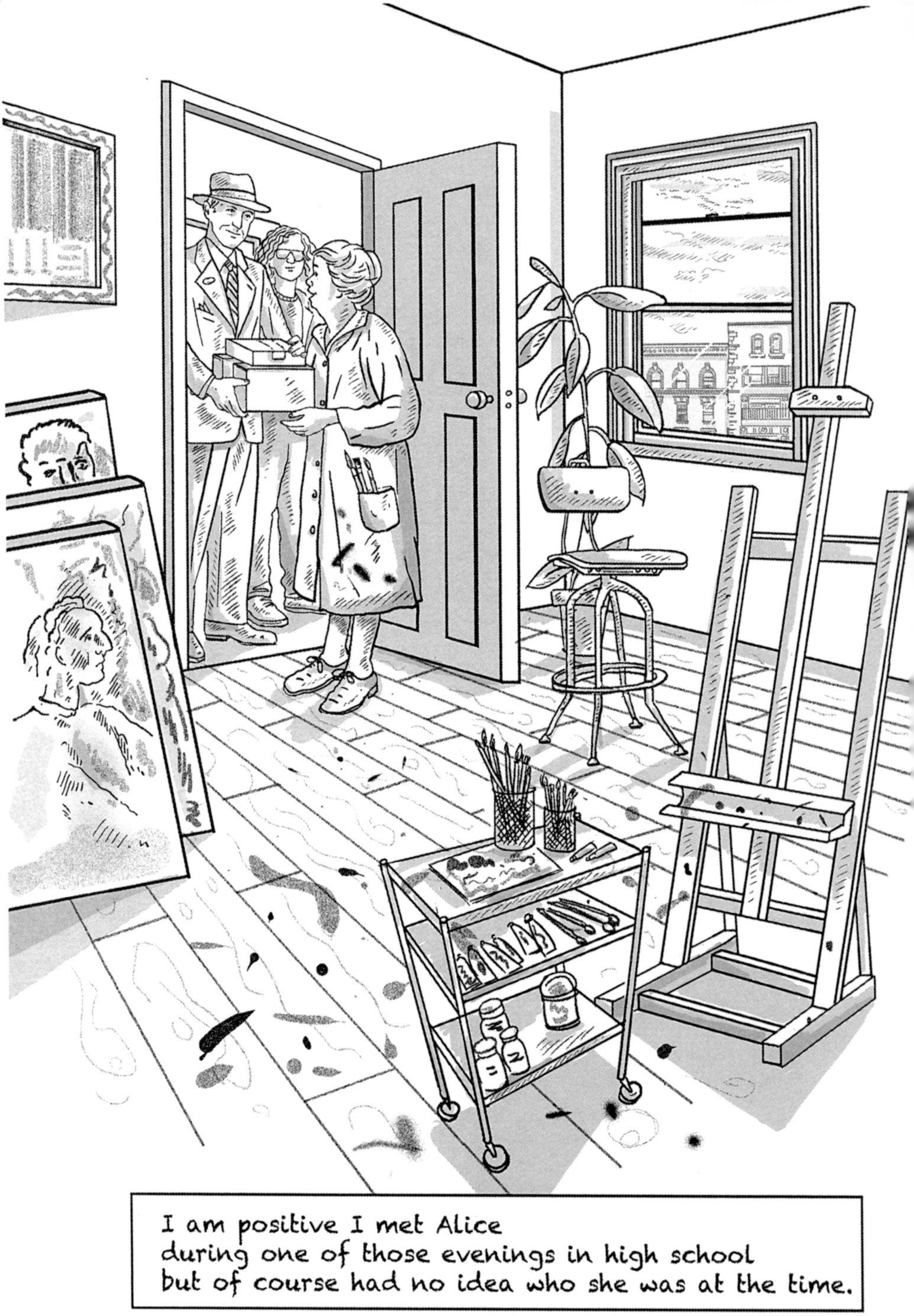
I am positive I met Alice
during one of those evenings in high school
but of course had no idea who she was at the time.

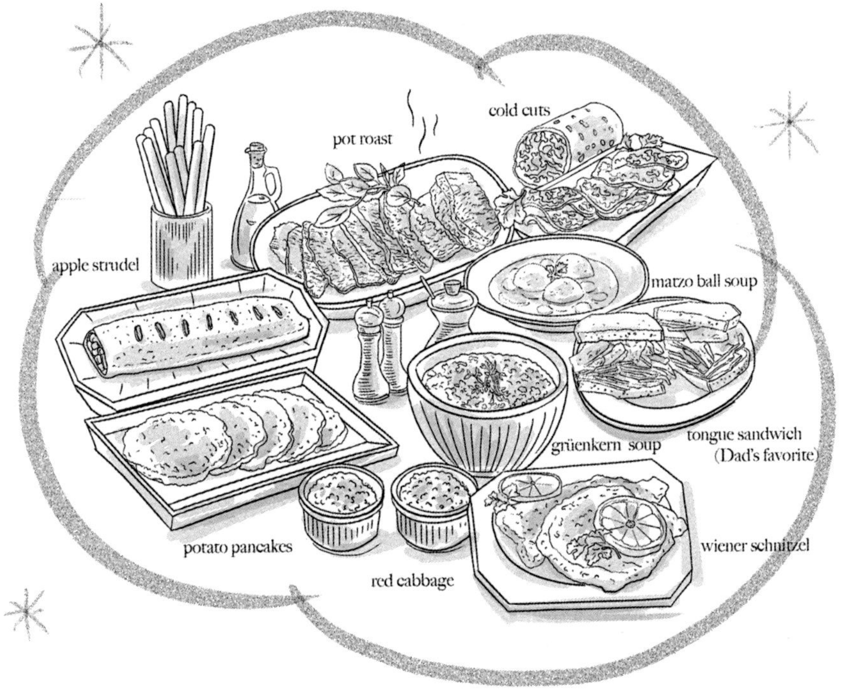
cold cuts
pot roast
apple strudel
matzo ball soup
tongue sandwich
(Dad's favorite)
grüenkern soup
potato pancakes
wiener schnitzel
red cabbage

I cherished those Friday evenings, tip money in hand, riding the 4 bus home with my Dad after a hard day's work,

looking forward to my Mom's delicious German-Jewish meals.

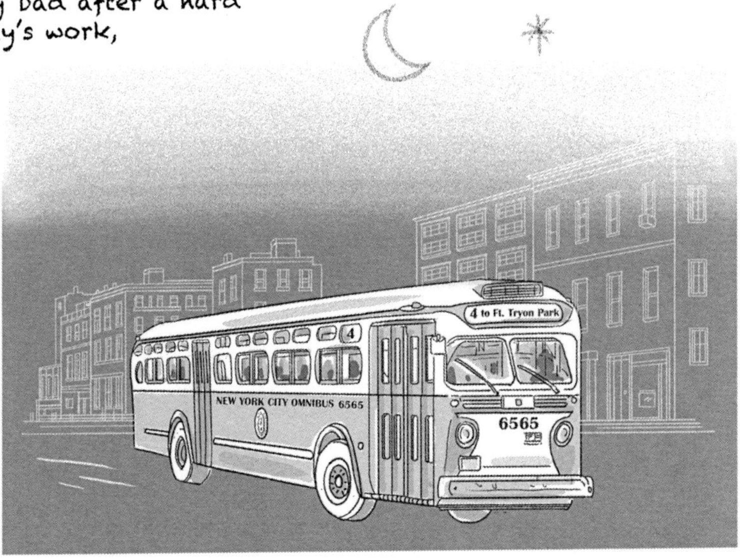
4 to Ft. Tryon Park
4
NEW YORK CITY OMNIBUS 6565
6565

Chapter 2:
First-Time View

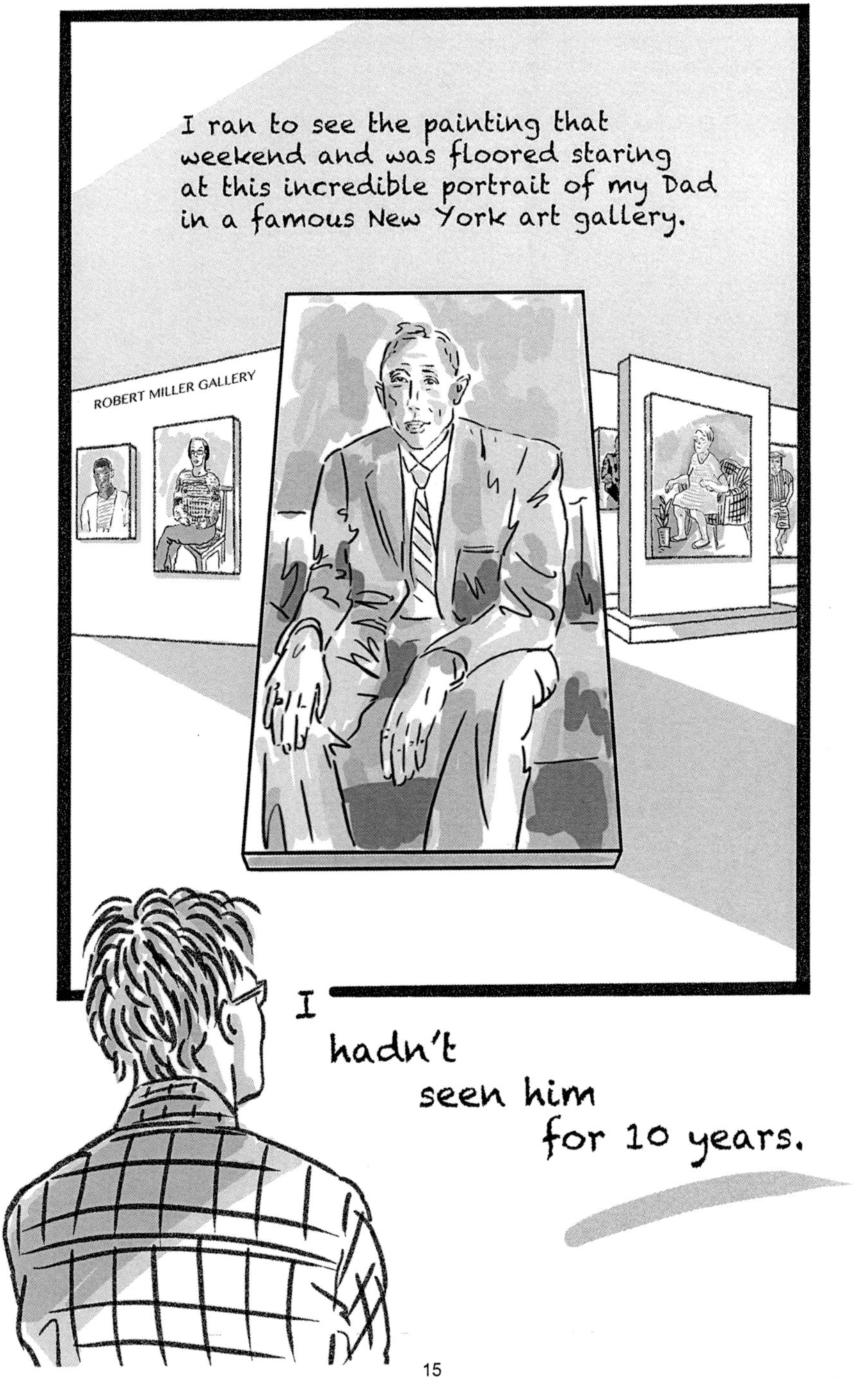
I ran to see the painting that weekend and was floored staring at this incredible portrait of my Dad in a famous New York art gallery.
ROBERT MILLER GALLERY
I hadn't seen him for 10 years.

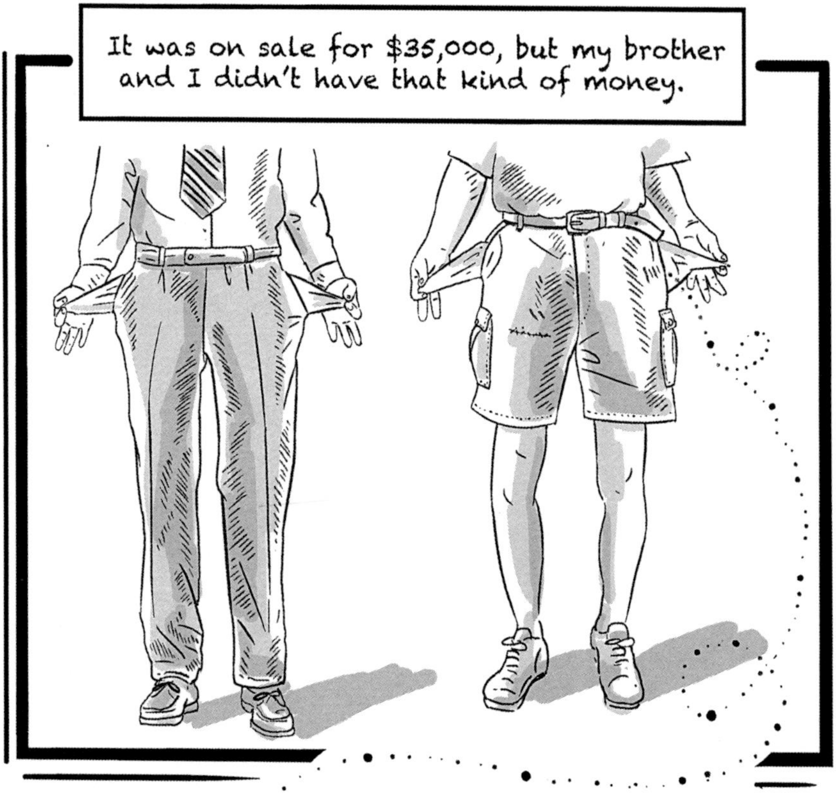
It was on sale for $35,000, but my brother and I didn't have that kind of money.

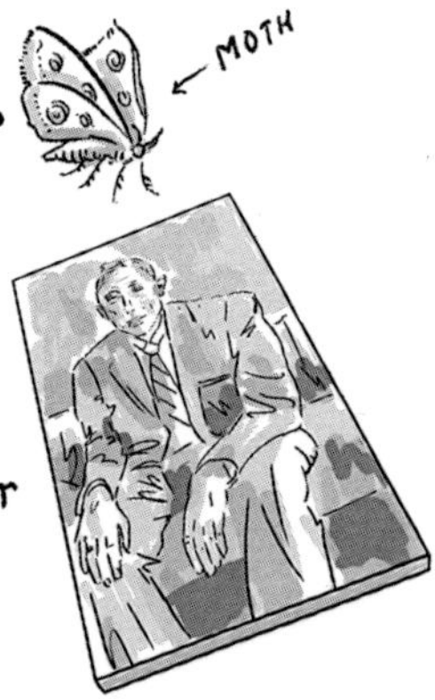
MOTH

My cousin
the doctor also saw the
painting that Sunday, considered
buying it, but didn't.

Of course, over the years, we had
countless discussions about whether
or not that was the right decision.

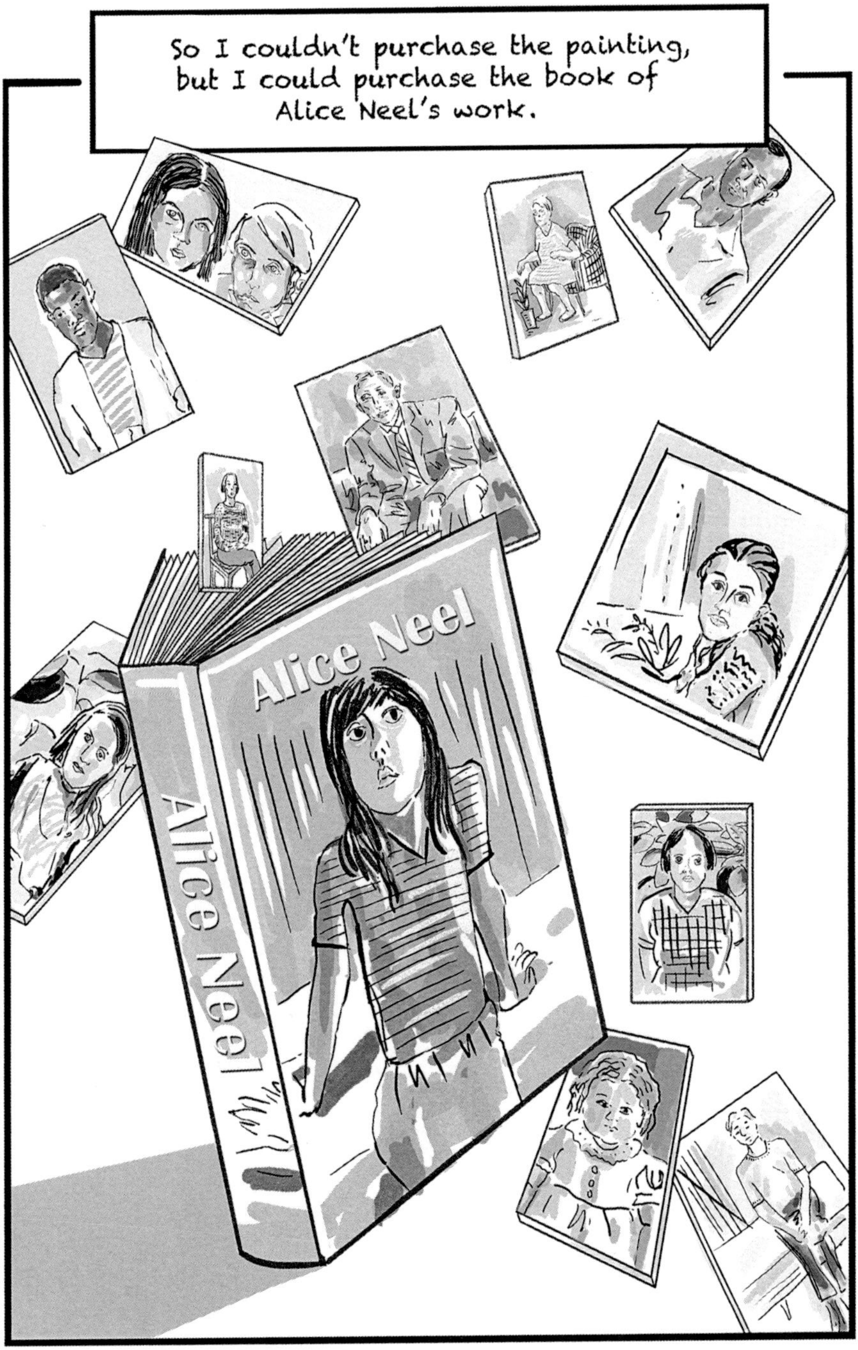
So I couldn't purchase the painting, but I could purchase the book of Alice Neel's work.
Alice Neel
Alice Neel

In it, my Dad was prominently featured: an anonymous Fuller Brush Man with a grin, someone who had escaped from Nazi Germany and survived Dachau.

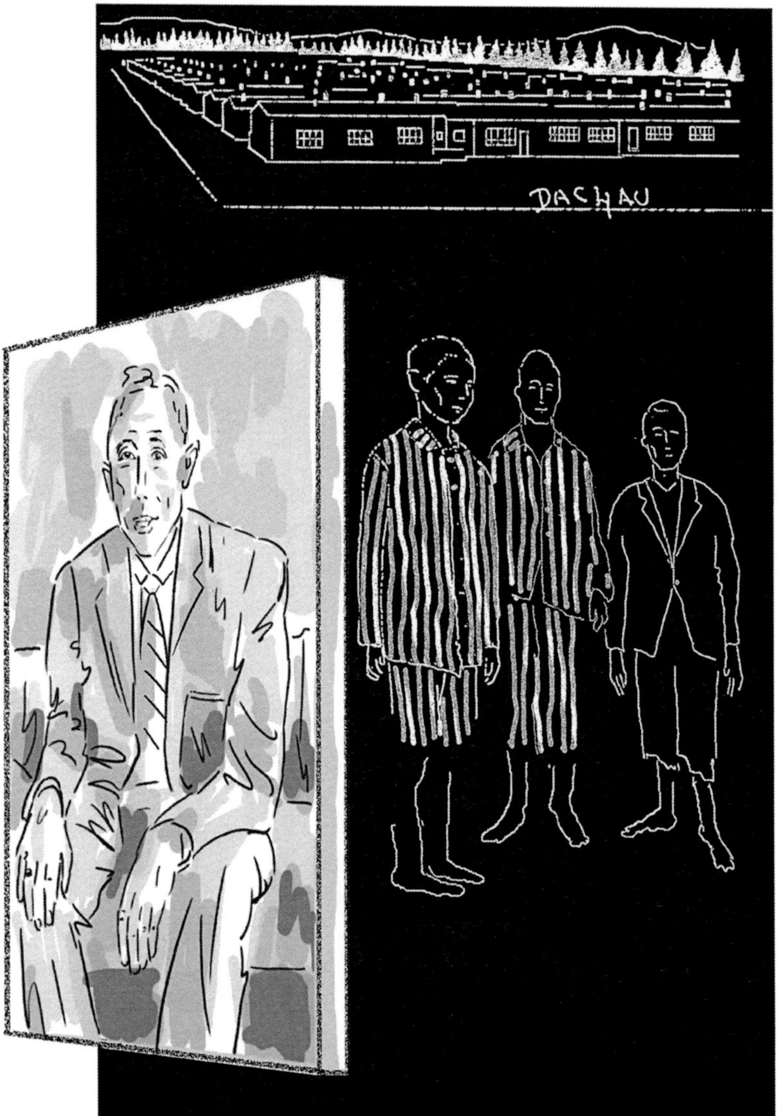
DACHAU

Chapter 3:
Alice and Dad

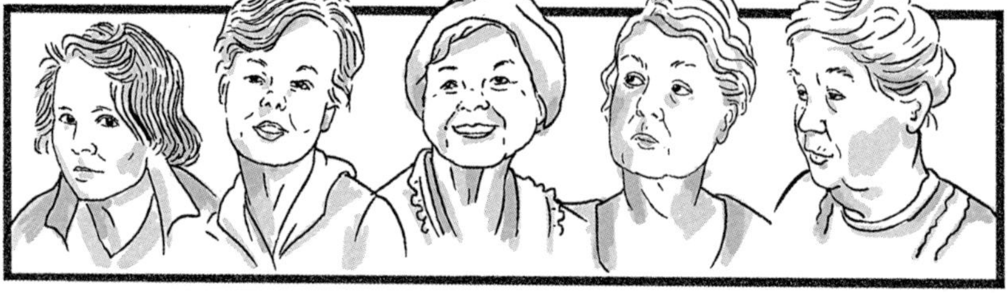

But what is the backstory behind Alice

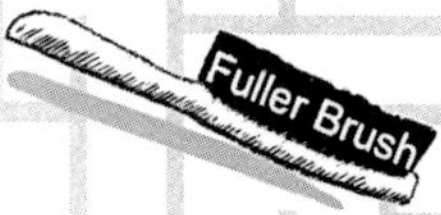

Fuller Brush

. . . and my Dad, Dewald Strauss?

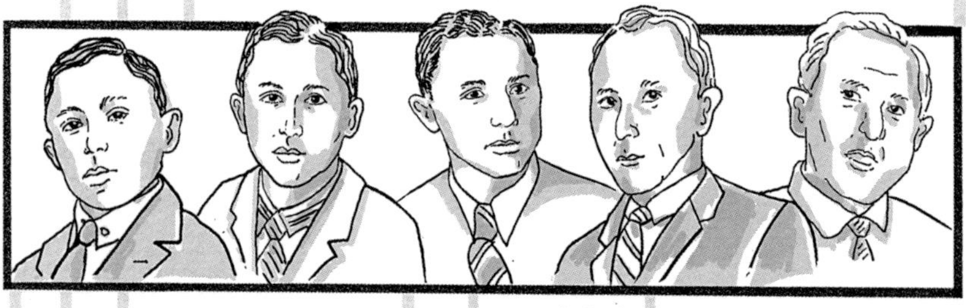

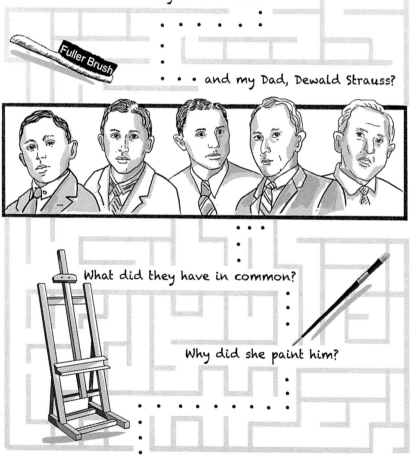

What did they have in common?

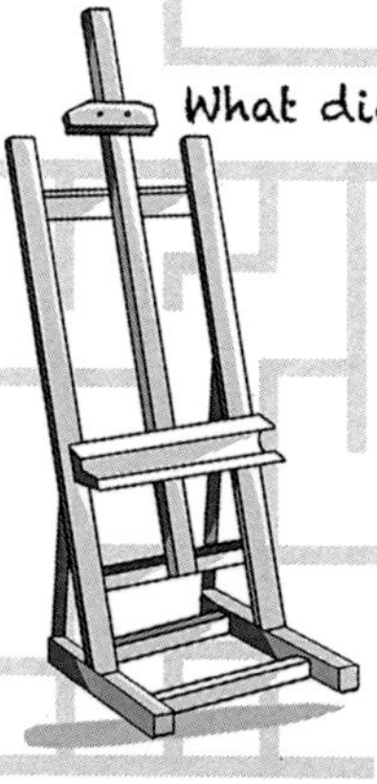

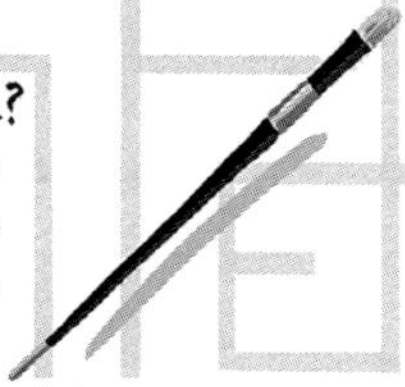

Why did she paint him?

How did the lives of Alice Neel and Dewald Strauss intersect?

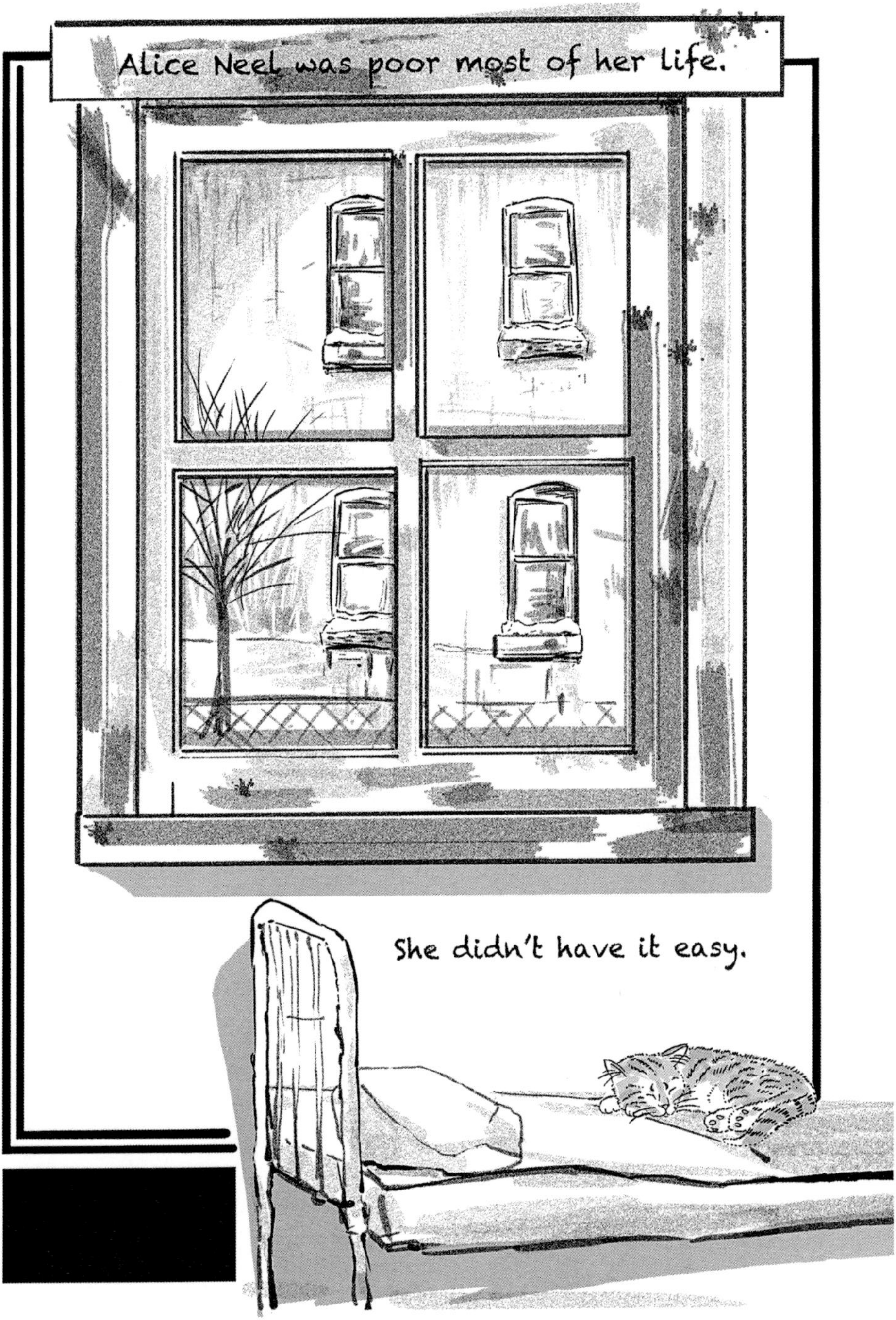
Alice Neel was poor most of her life.
She didn't have it easy.

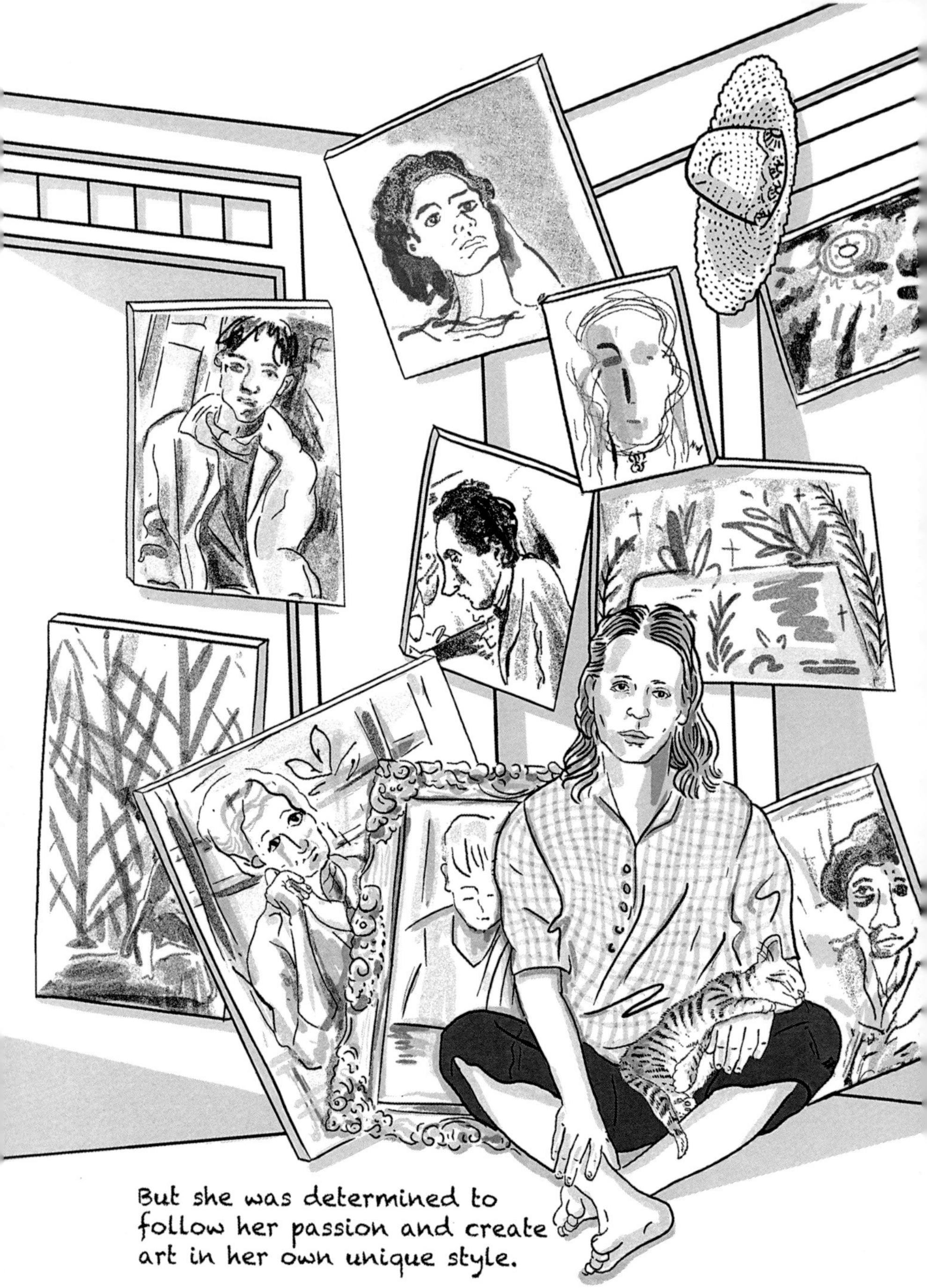
But she was determined to
follow her passion and create
art in her own unique style.

She lived among others of a similar background, people living on the edge of society.

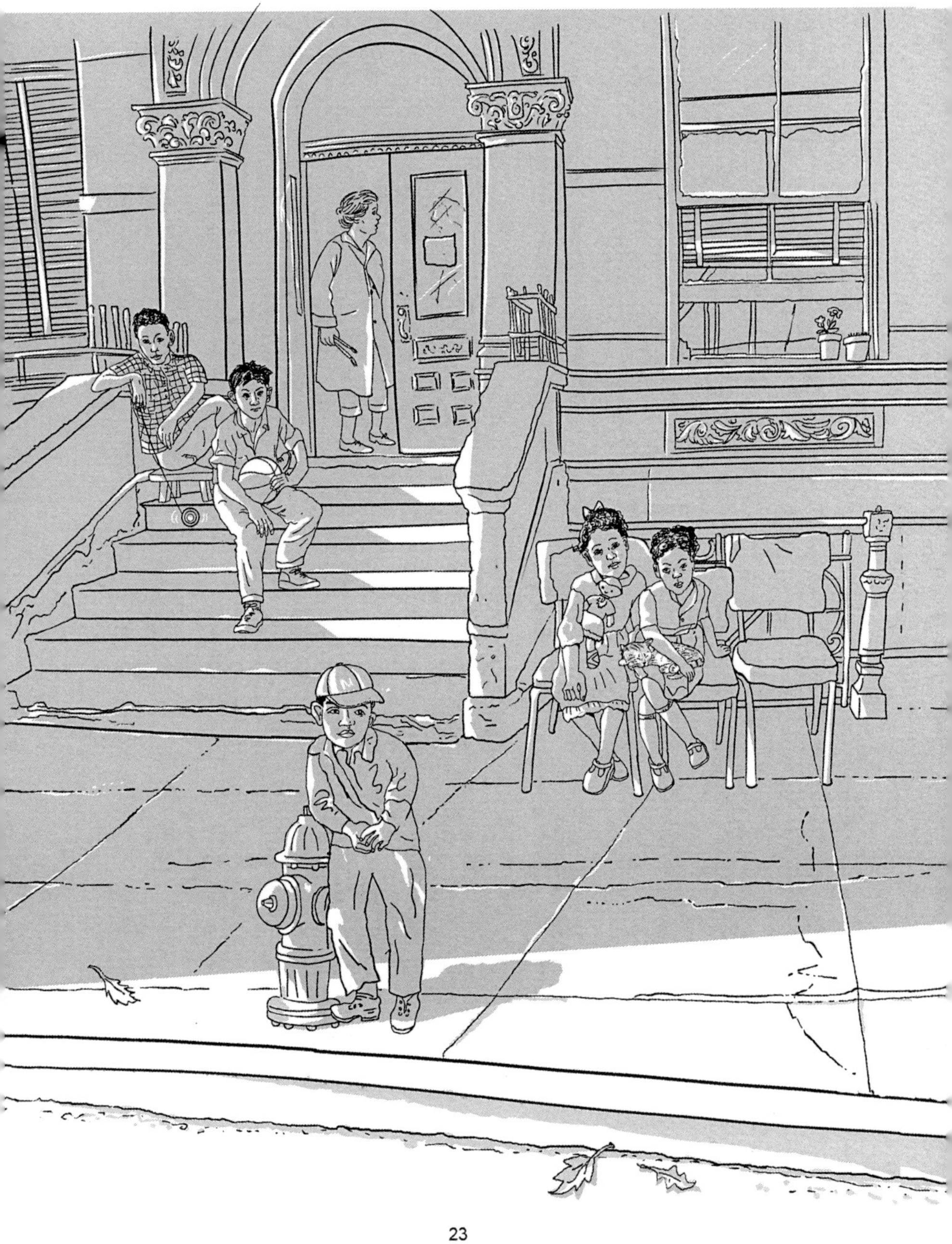

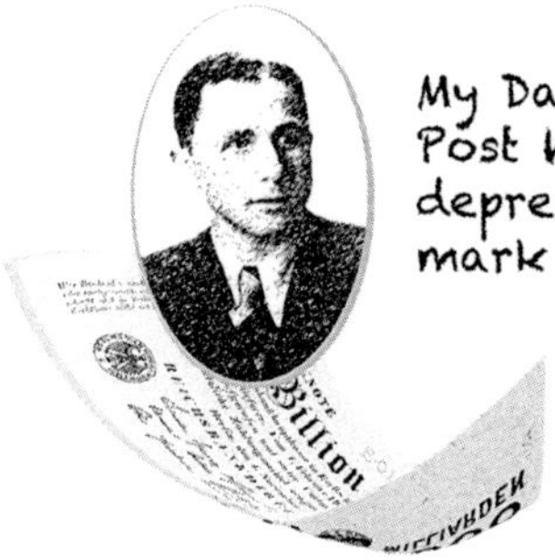

My Dad grew up in the '20s in Germany. Post World War I was a time of economic depression and hyperinflation, with billion mark bills being used as *tissue paper.*

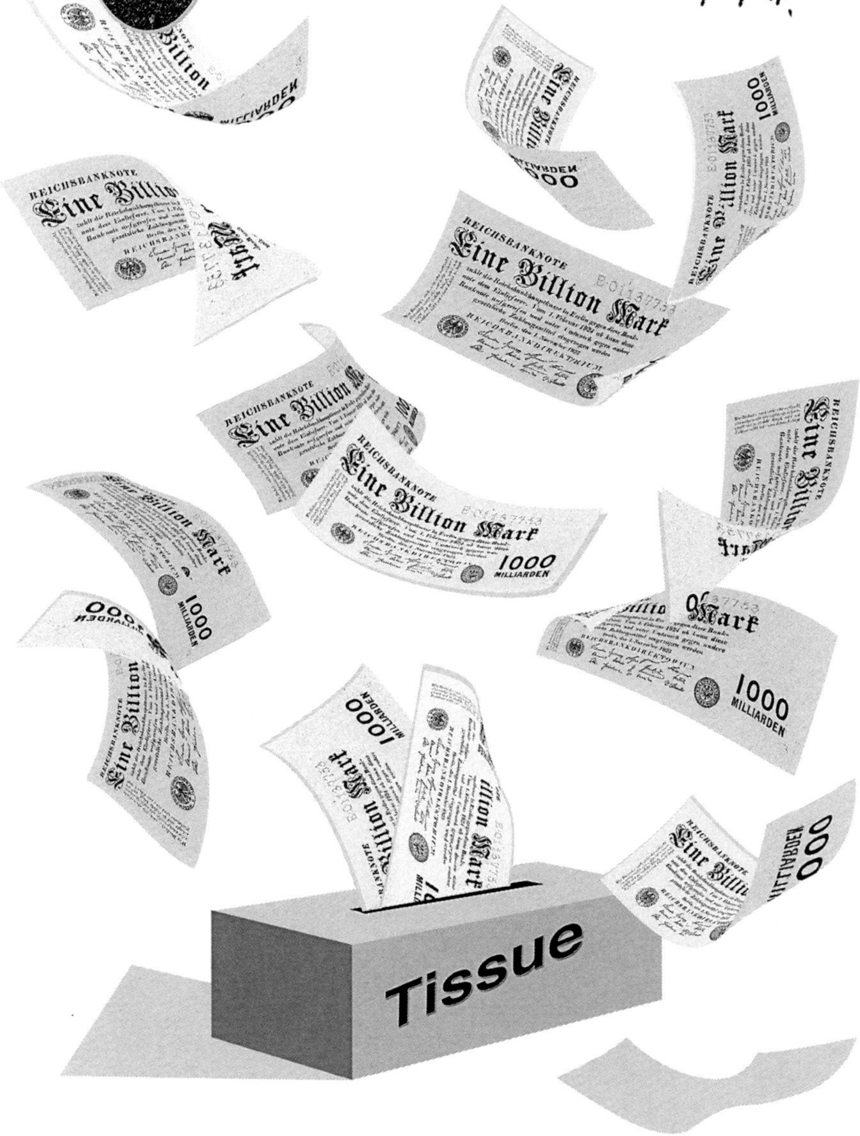
REICHSBANKNOTE
Eine Billion Mark
1000
MILLIARDEN
Tissue

In the early '30s, as a German Jew, he was an assimilated middle-class textile salesman, making a good living, practicing his religion, and living in relative freedom.

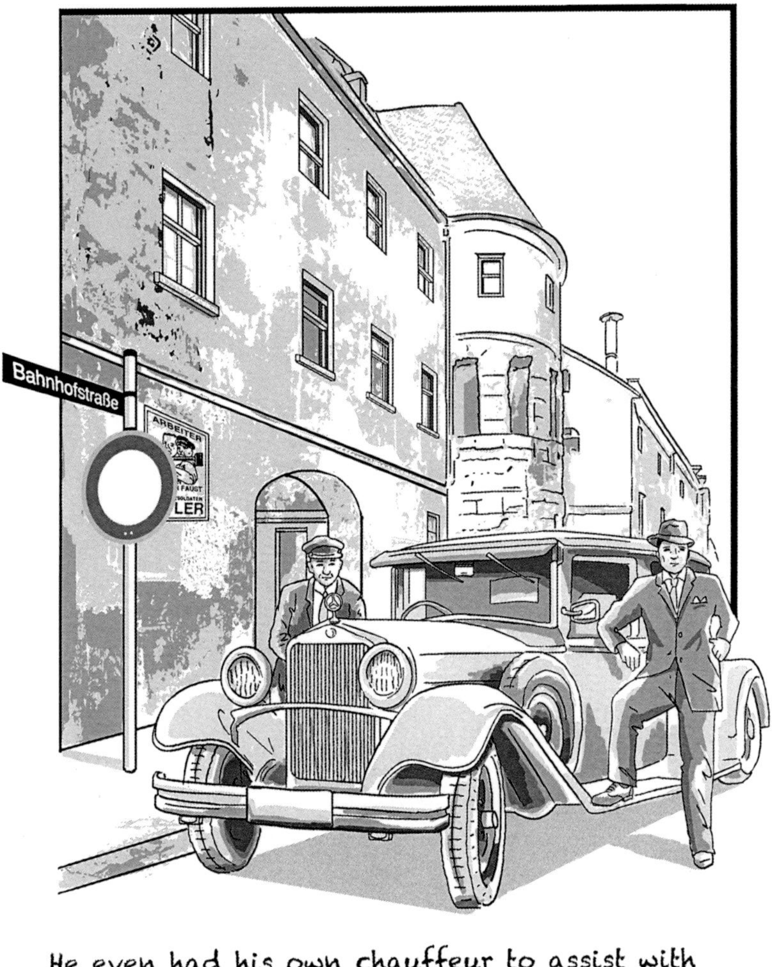
Bahnhofstraße
ARBEITER

He even had his own chauffeur to assist with carrying heavy samples and rushing him from customer to customer.

However, by the '30s, the Nazis came to power and there was rampant antisemitism in the country.

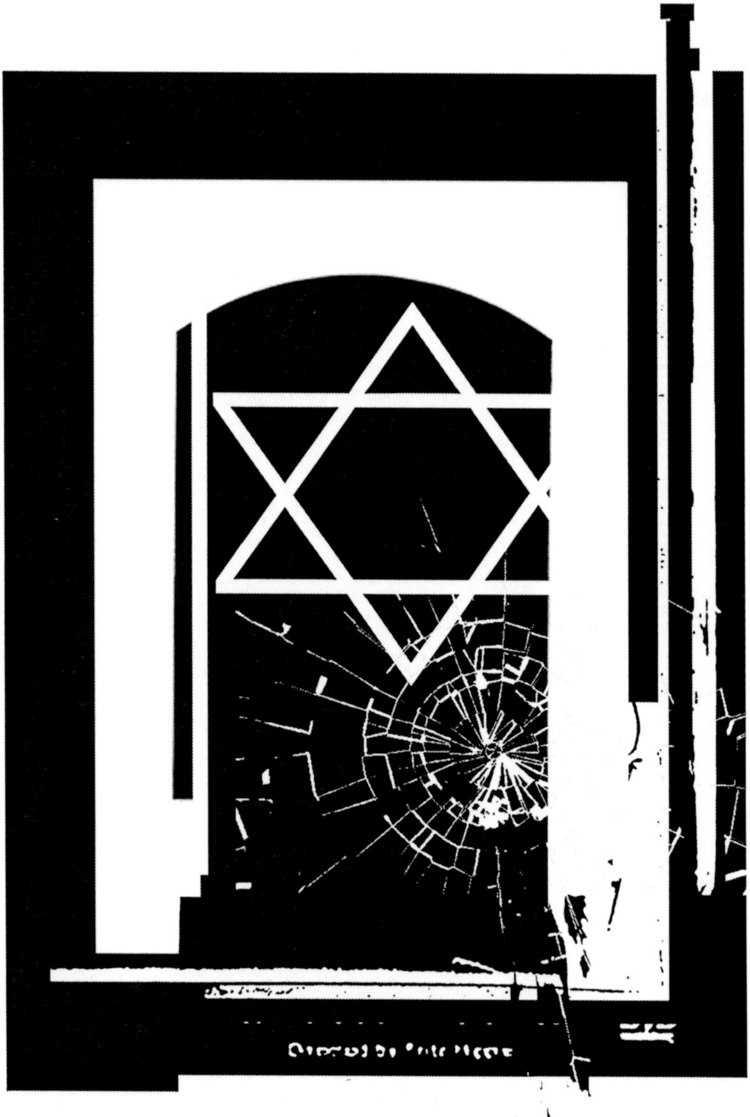

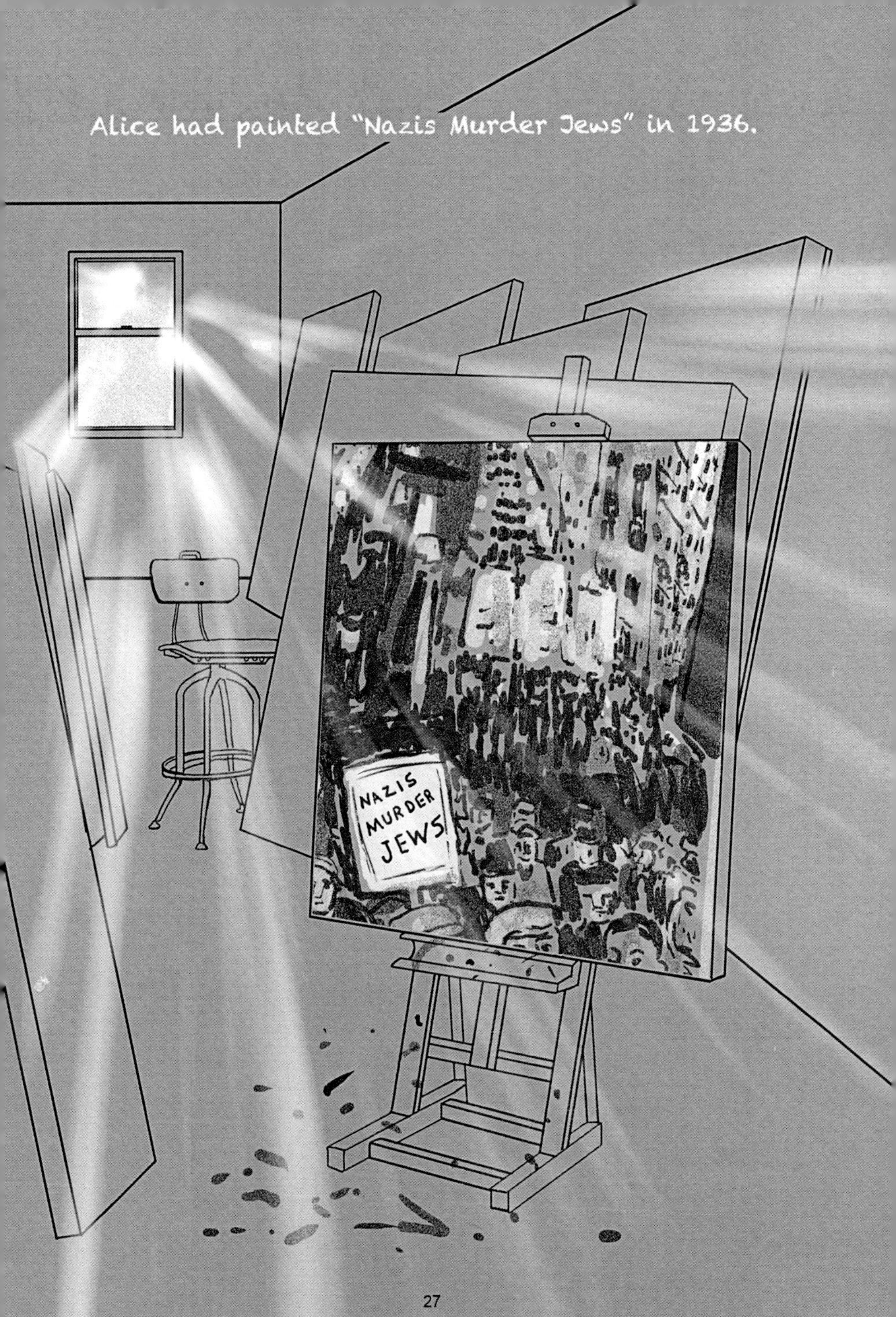
Alice had painted "Nazis Murder Jews" in 1936.
NAZIS MURDER JEWS

Chapter 4:
Deportation to Dachau

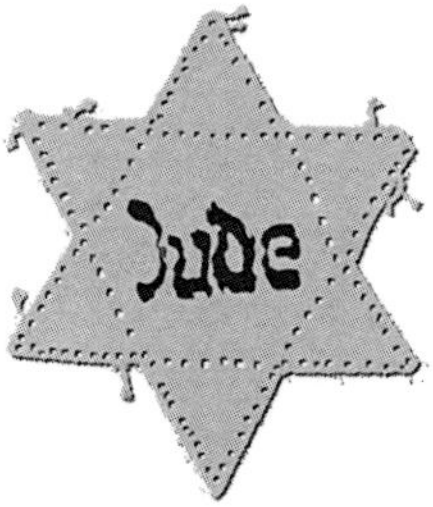
Jude

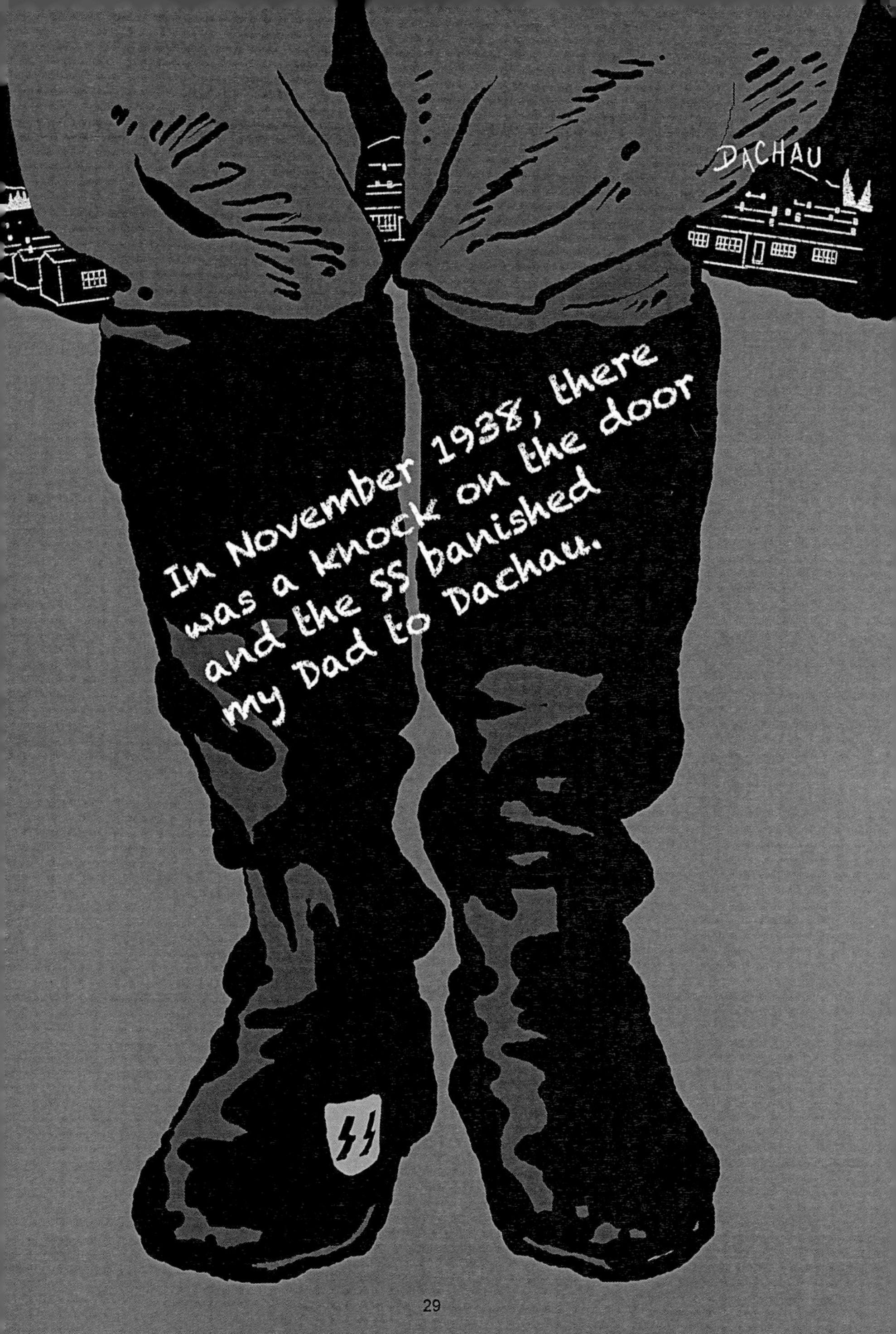
DACHAU
In November 1938, there
was a knock on the door
and the SS banished
my Dad to Dachau.

This original Nazi ledger indicates that he was prisoner 20,139, born in Billigheim, single, no children, a Jew, a salesman living in Regensburg.

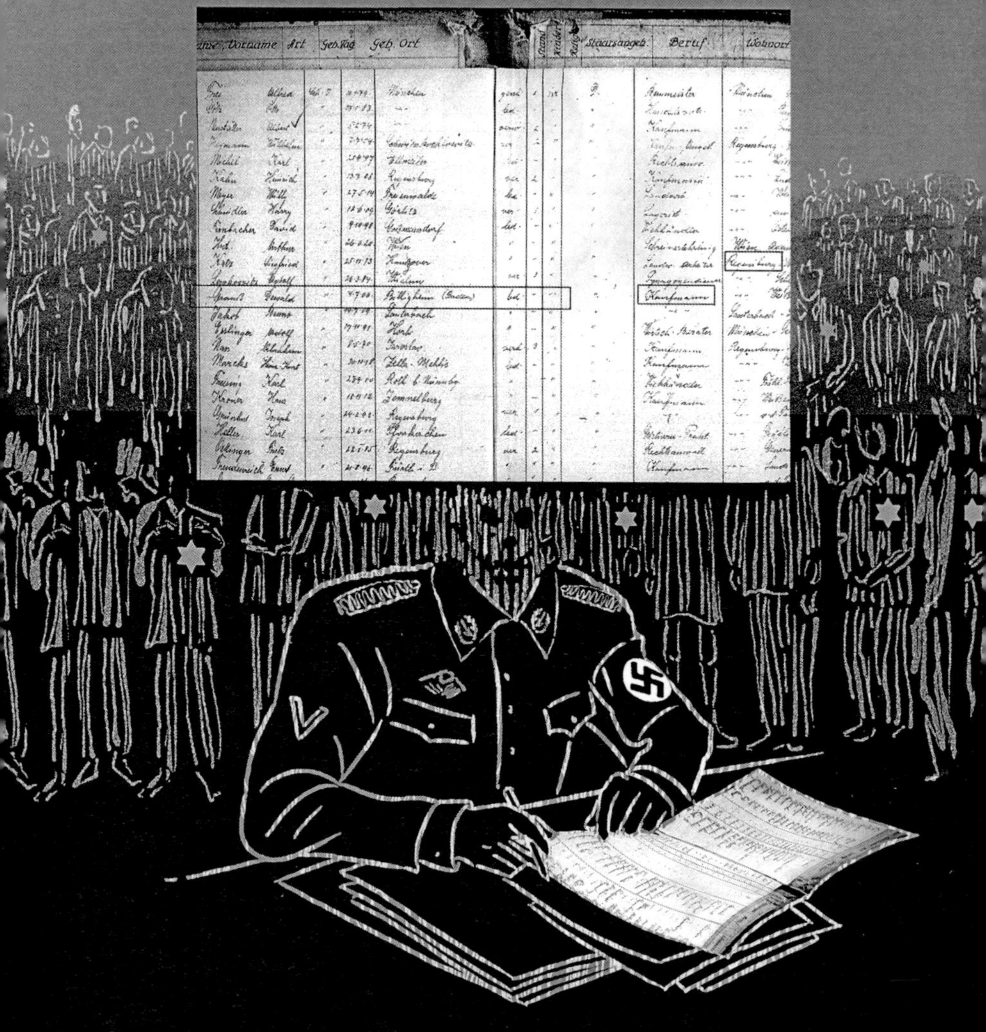
Vorname
Art
Geb.Tag
Geb. Ort
Staatsangeh.
Beruf
Wohnort

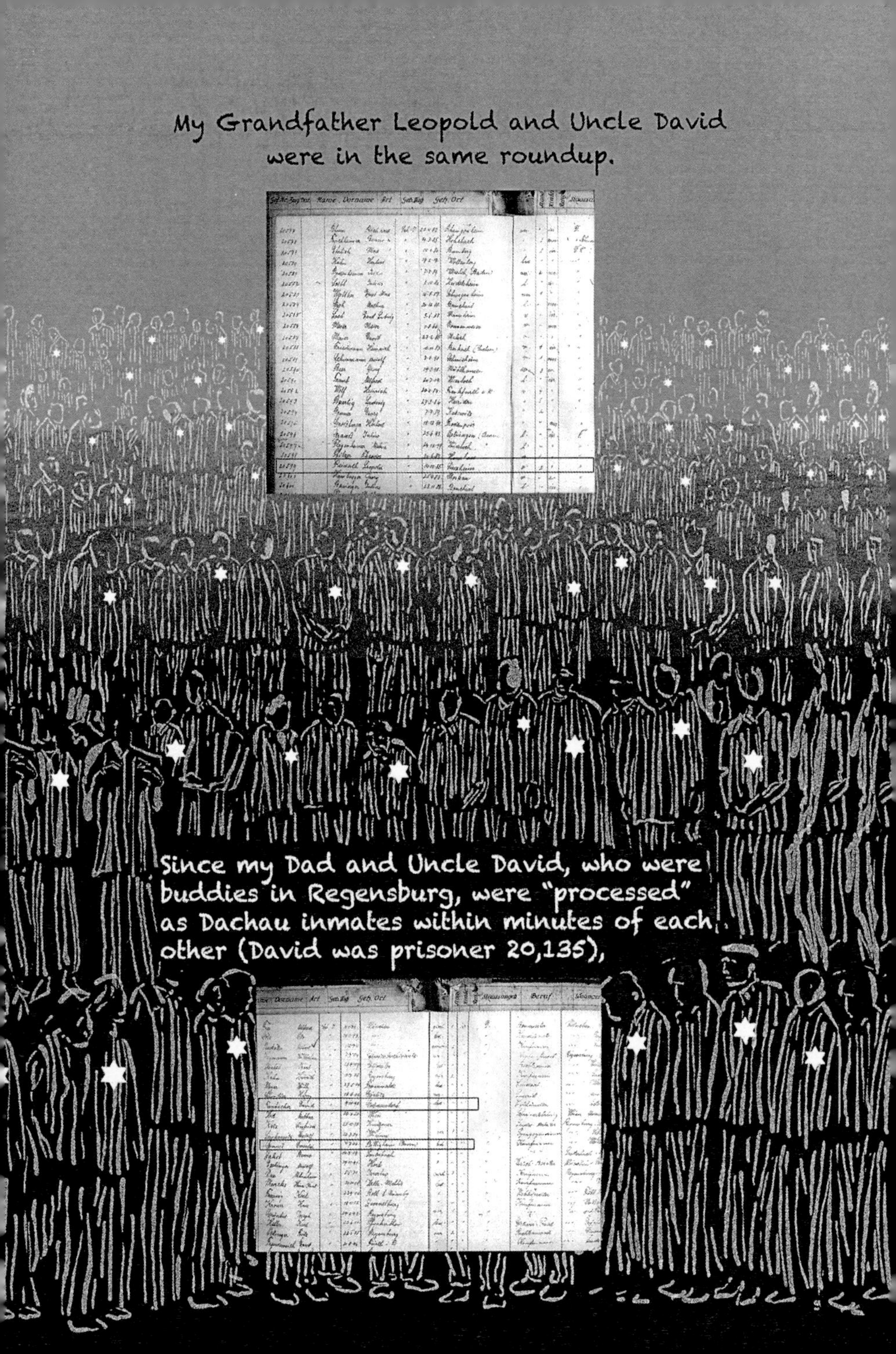
My Grandfather Leopold and Uncle David were in the same roundup.
Since my Dad and Uncle David, who were buddies in Regensburg, were "processed" as Dachau inmates within minutes of each other (David was prisoner 20,135),

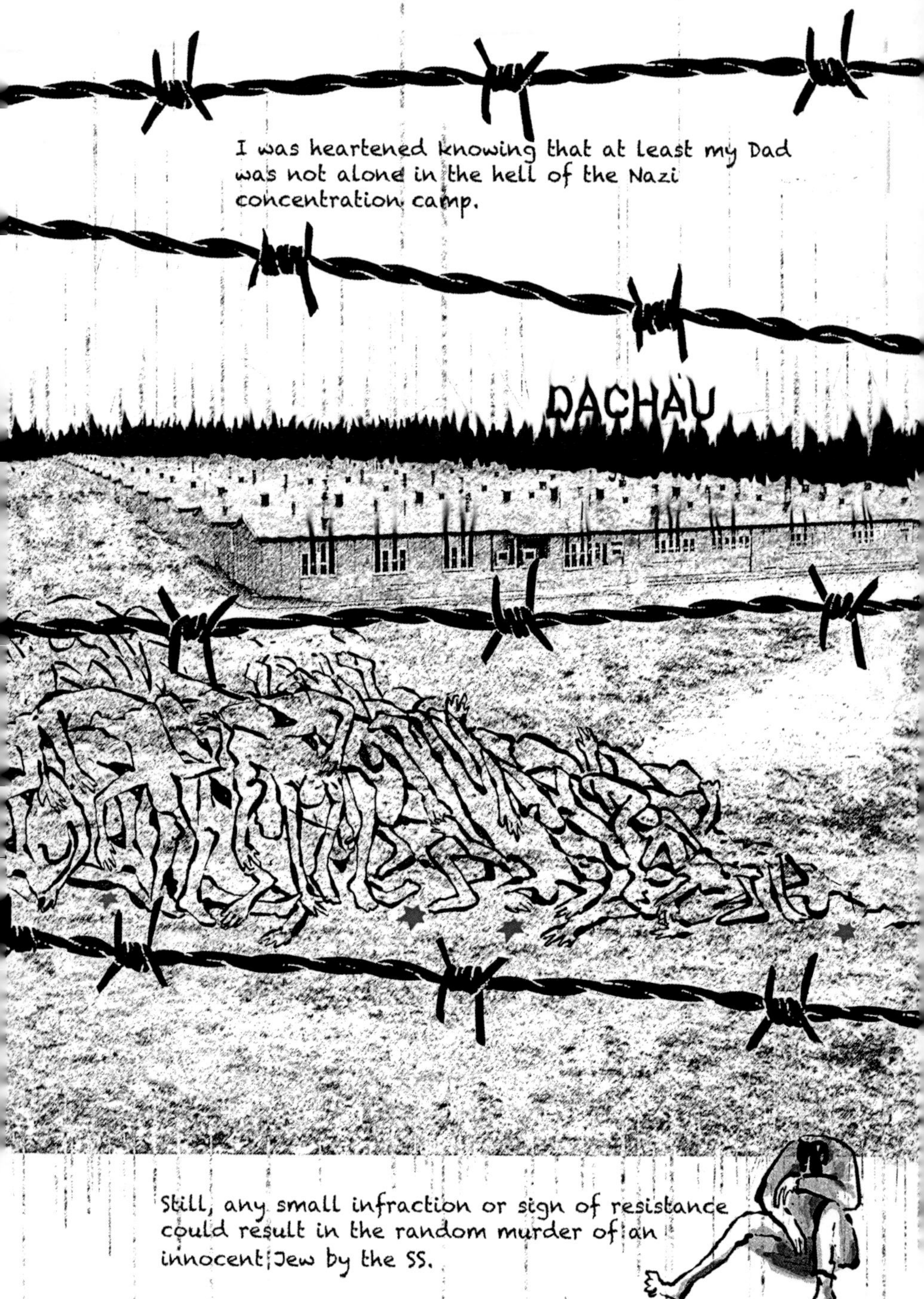
I was heartened knowing that at least my Dad was not alone in the hell of the Nazi concentration camp.
DACHAU
Still, any small infraction or sign of resistance could result in the random murder of an innocent Jew by the SS.

I learned these details through my own research,
but the one thing my Dad mentioned to me
about Dachau was that he burned all his clothes
when he got home since they were full of lice.

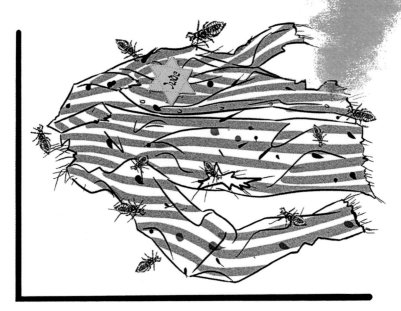

Wehrnummer
Regensburg
Polizeil. Meldebehörde
Regensburg
Wehrbezirkskommando
Regensburg
Ausschließungsschein
wird hiermit vom Dienst in der Wehrmacht im Frieden
ausgeschlossen.
Regensburg
Die Kreispolizeibehörde
Der Wehrbezirkskommandeur
Zur Beachtung

certificate of exclusion

Chapter 5:
The Other Alice –
Escape to Freedom

That's where my Dad's sister came into the picture. He was able to enter the States with the help of my Aunt, also named Alice, and her affidavit.

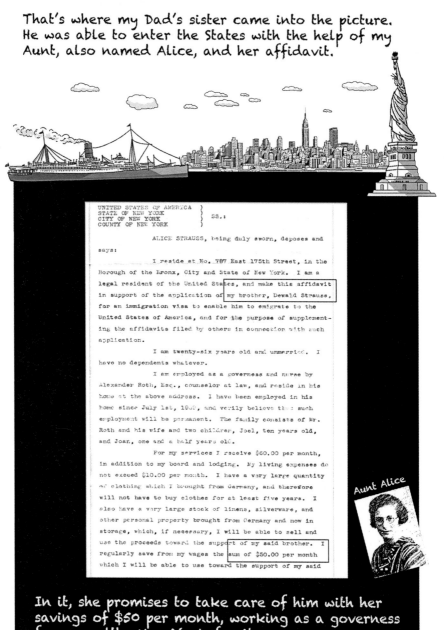

UNITED STATES OF AMERICA)
STATE OF NEW YORK)
CITY OF NEW YORK) SS.:
COUNTY OF NEW YORK)

ALICE STRAUSS, being duly sworn, deposes and says:

I reside at No. 787 East 175th Street, in the Borough of the Bronx, City and State of New York. I am a legal resident of the United States, and make this affidavit in support of the application of my brother, Dewald Strauss, for an immigration visa to enable him to emigrate to the United States of America, and for the purpose of supplementing the affidavits filed by others in connection with such application.

I am twenty-six years old and unmarried. I have no dependents whatever.

I am employed as a governess and nurse by Alexander Roth, Esq., counselor at law, and reside in his home at the above address. I have been employed in his home since July 1st, 1909, and verily believe that such employment will be permanent. The family consists of Mr. Roth and his wife and two children, Joel, ten years old, and Joan, one and a half years old.

For my services I receive $60.00 per month, in addition to my board and lodging. My living expenses do not exceed $10.00 per month. I have a very large quantity of clothing which I brought from Germany, and therefore will not have to buy clothes for at least five years. I also have a very large stock of linens, silverware, and other personal property brought from Germany and now in storage, which, if necessary, I will be able to sell and use the proceeds toward the support of my said brother. I regularly save from my wages the sum of $50.00 per month which I will be able to use toward the support of my said

Aunt Alice

In it, she promises to take care of him with her savings of $50 per month, working as a governess for a wealthy New York family.

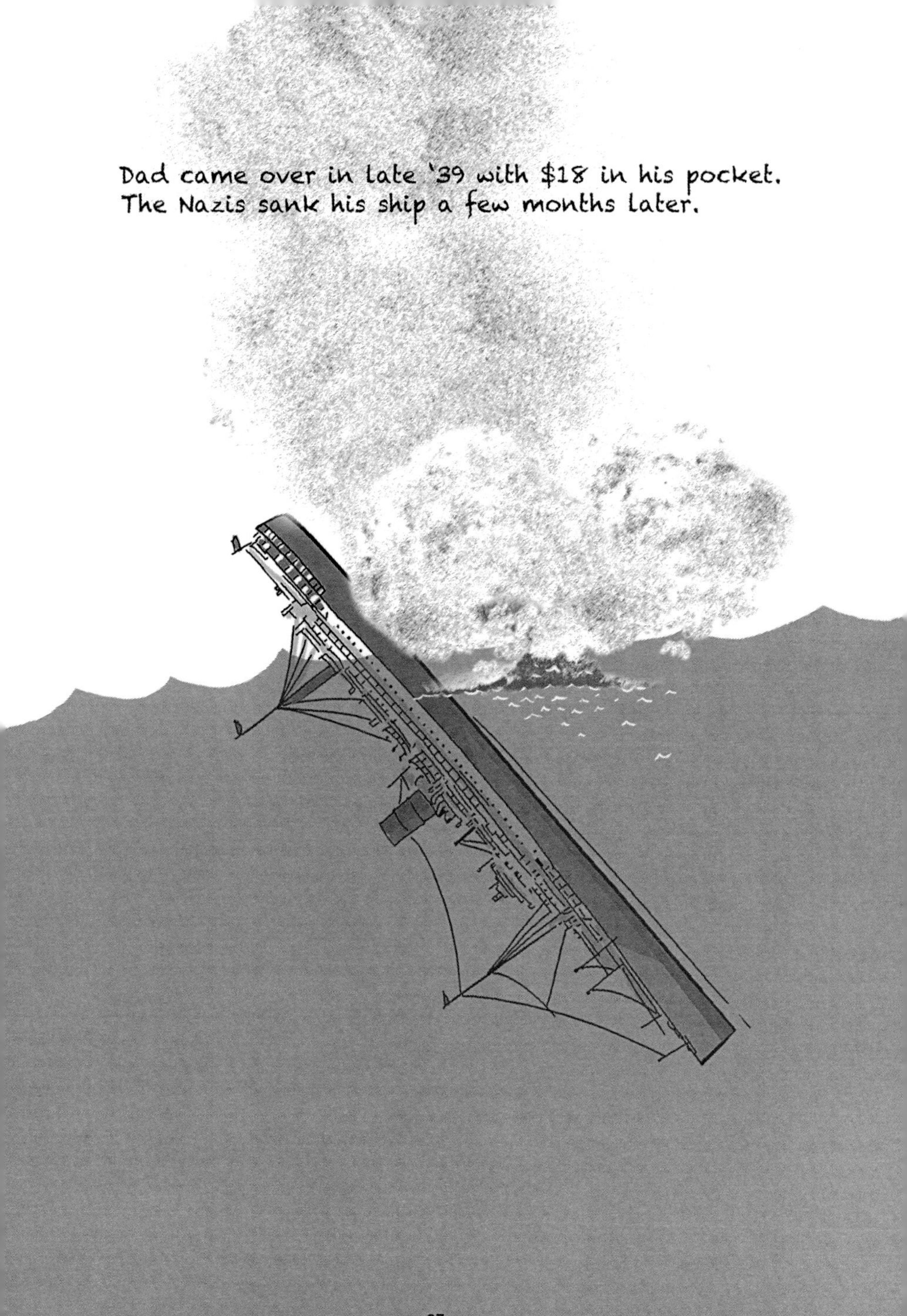
Dad came over in late '39 with $18 in his pocket.
The Nazis sank his ship a few months later.

His first job was at the 1939–1940 NY World's Fair as a busboy. It was a far cry from his lucrative traveling salesman's job in Europe, but he was safe.

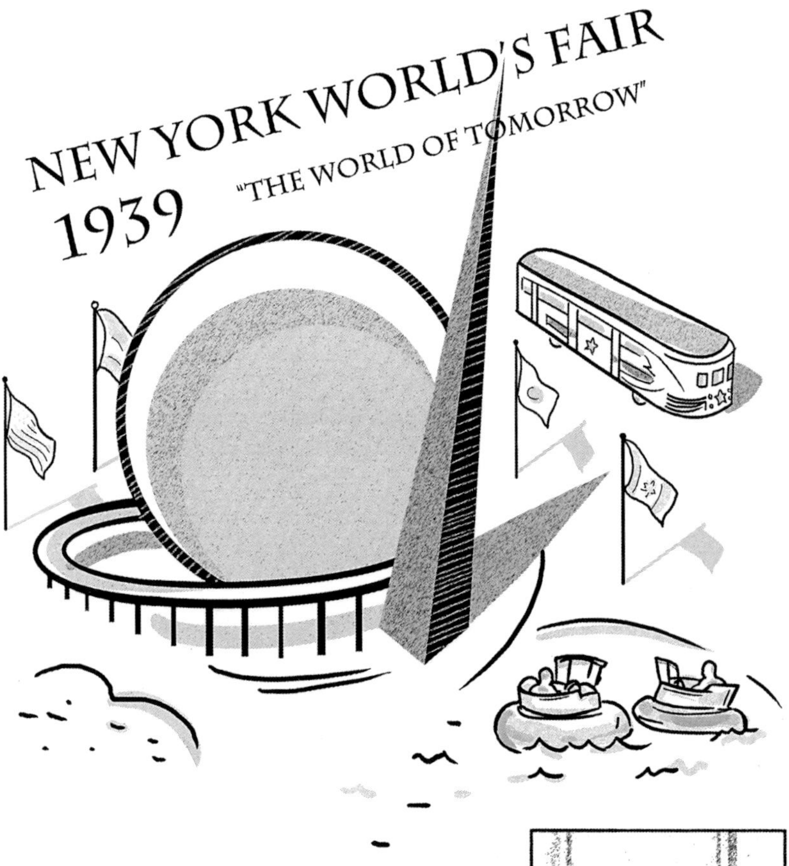
NEW YORK WORLD'S FAIR
1939
"THE WORLD OF TOMORROW"

That's my Mom at the World's Fair with my Uncle Carl. Although my folks grew up in different towns within a short distance of Heidelberg and crossed paths at the Fair, they didn't meet until after the War.

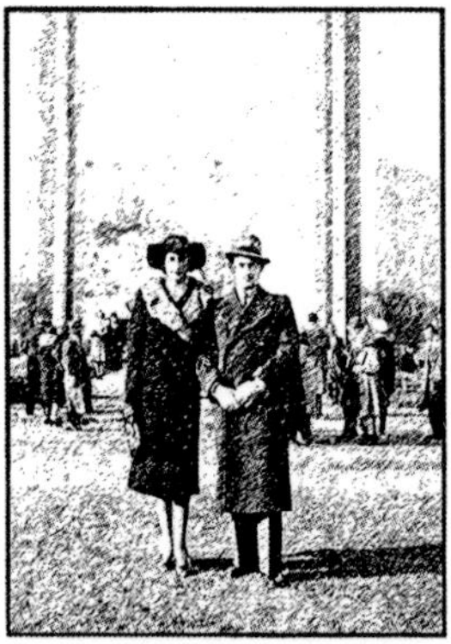

Chapter 6:
The War

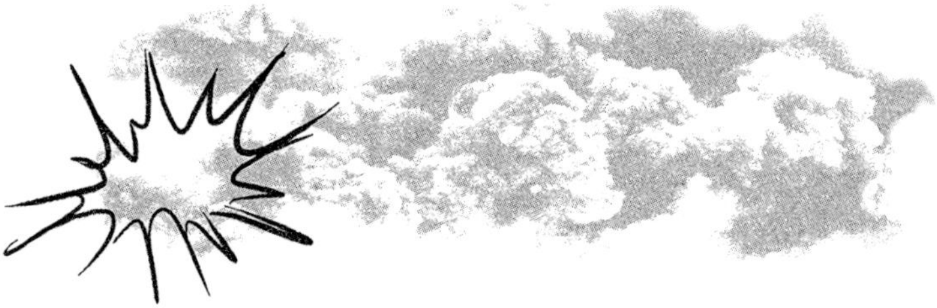

After Pearl Harbor, my Dad entered the Army.
He was inducted in 1942 and landed in Europe just in time for the Battle of the Bulge.
He was wounded by shrapnel, endured multiple operations and sent right back to the front when he healed. I remember seeing his scars.

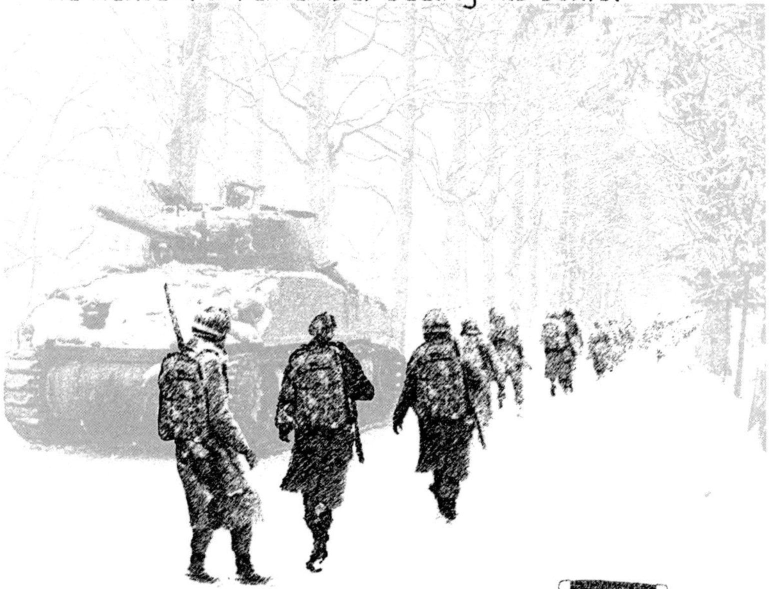

He was injured in Andernach, only 250 kilometers from where he was born.
We still have his Purple Heart.

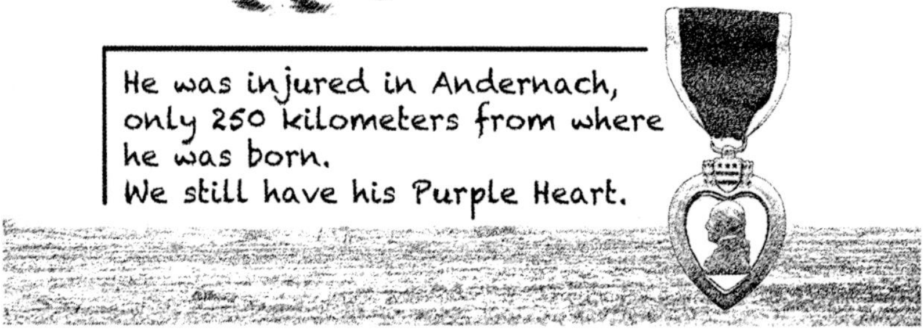

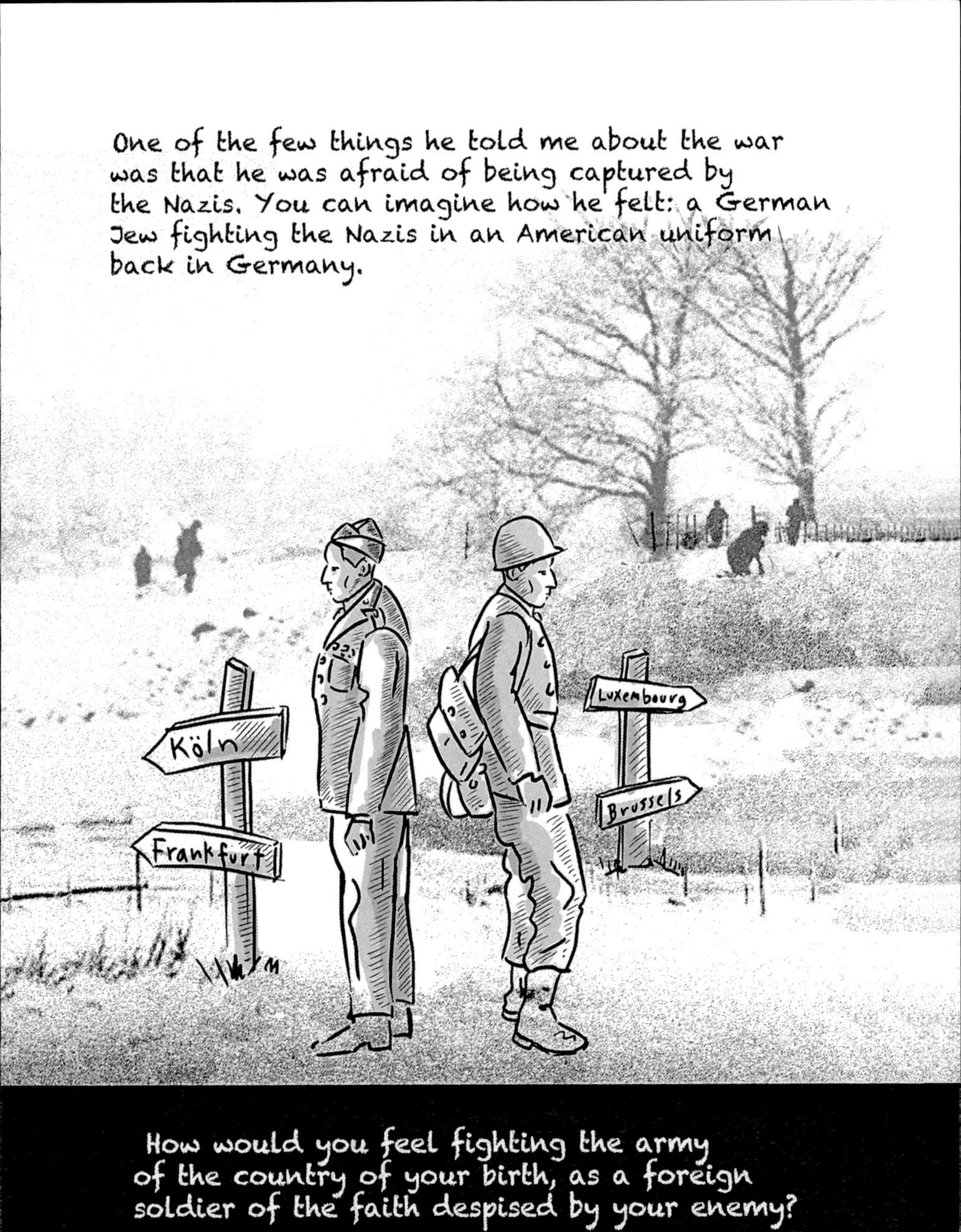
One of the few things he told me about the war was that he was afraid of being captured by the Nazis. You can imagine how he felt: a German Jew fighting the Nazis in an American uniform back in Germany.
Köln
Frankfurt
Luxembourg
Brussels
How would you feel fighting the army of the country of your birth, as a foreign soldier of the faith despised by your enemy?

Chapter 7:
Fuller Brush Man - The Job

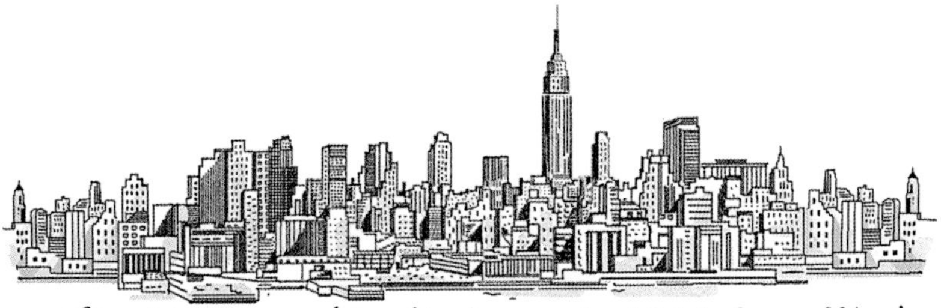

After his honorable discharge in 1946, he settled down in New York City and got back to what he knew best: selling.

So he became a Fuller Brush Man.

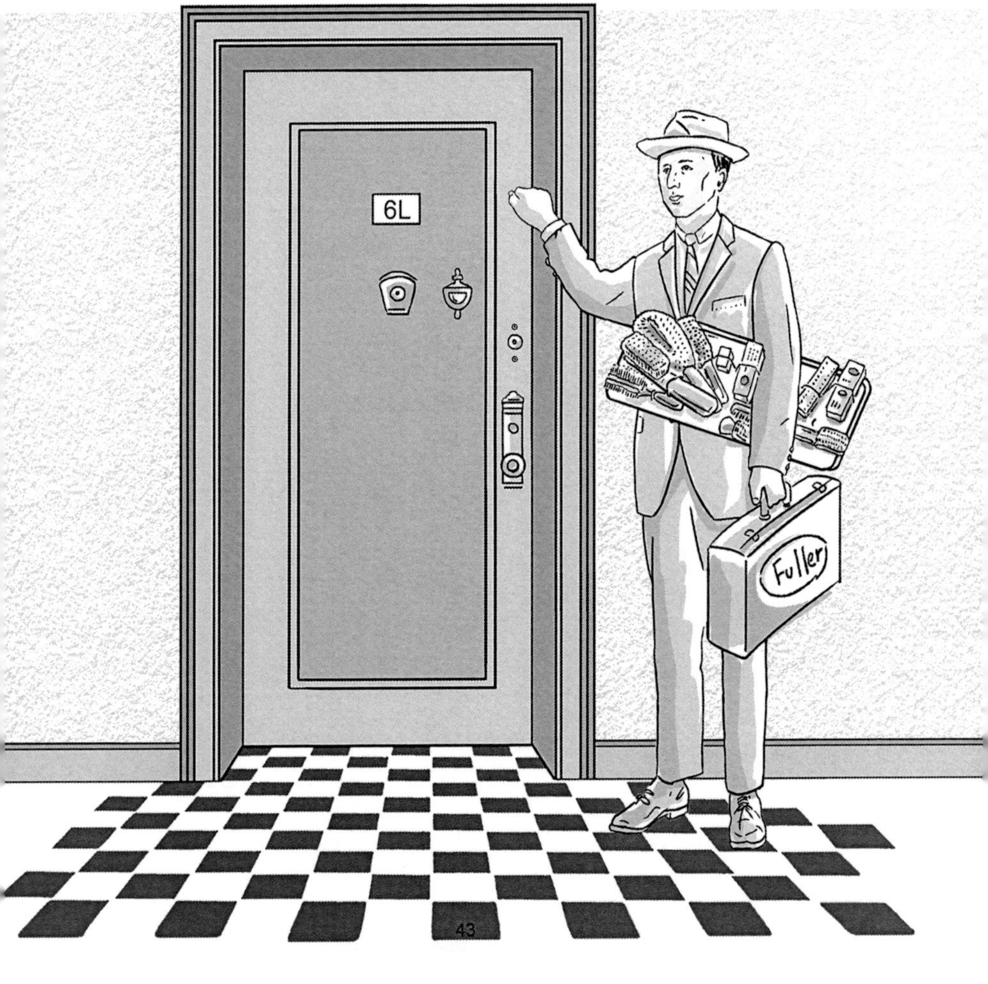
6L
Fuller

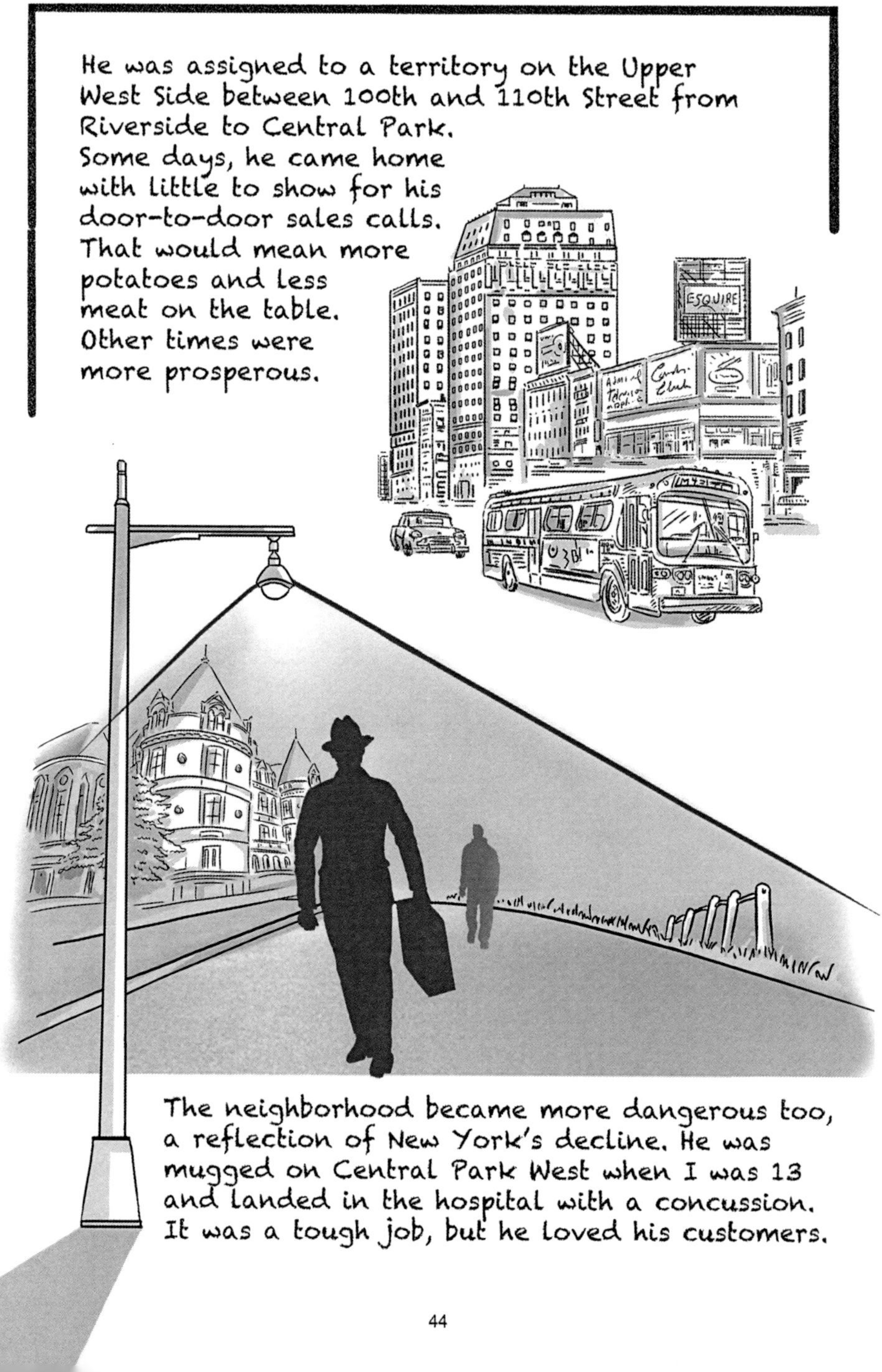
He was assigned to a territory on the Upper West Side between 100th and 110th Street from Riverside to Central Park. Some days, he came home with little to show for his door-to-door sales calls. That would mean more potatoes and less meat on the table. Other times were more prosperous.
ESQUIRE
The neighborhood became more dangerous too, a reflection of New York's decline. He was mugged on Central Park West when I was 13 and landed in the hospital with a concussion. It was a tough job, but he loved his customers.

Chapter 8:
The Rise of Alice

Although she was unknown in 1965 when she painted my Dad, in 1974 Alice had her first show at the Whitney, the same year my Dad died.

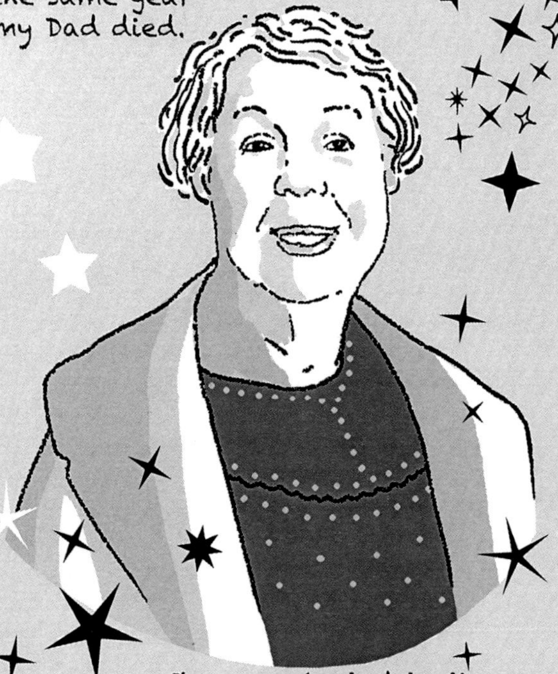

She was elected to the American Academy of Arts and Letters, the highest formal recognition of artistic merit in the US, and received the International Women's Year Award in 1976. But he never knew of her growing fame.

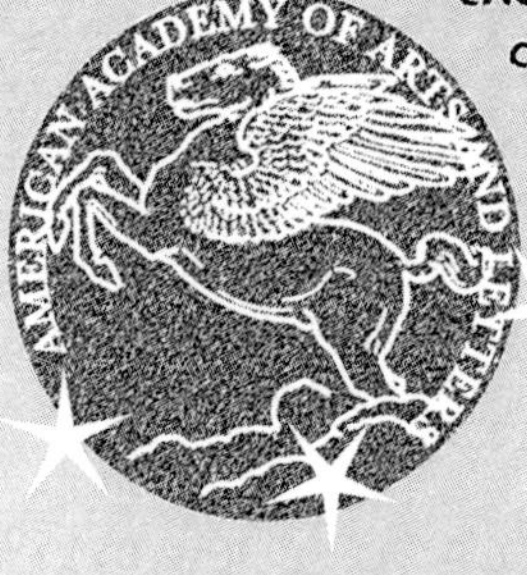
AMERICAN ACADEMY OF ARTS AND LETTERS

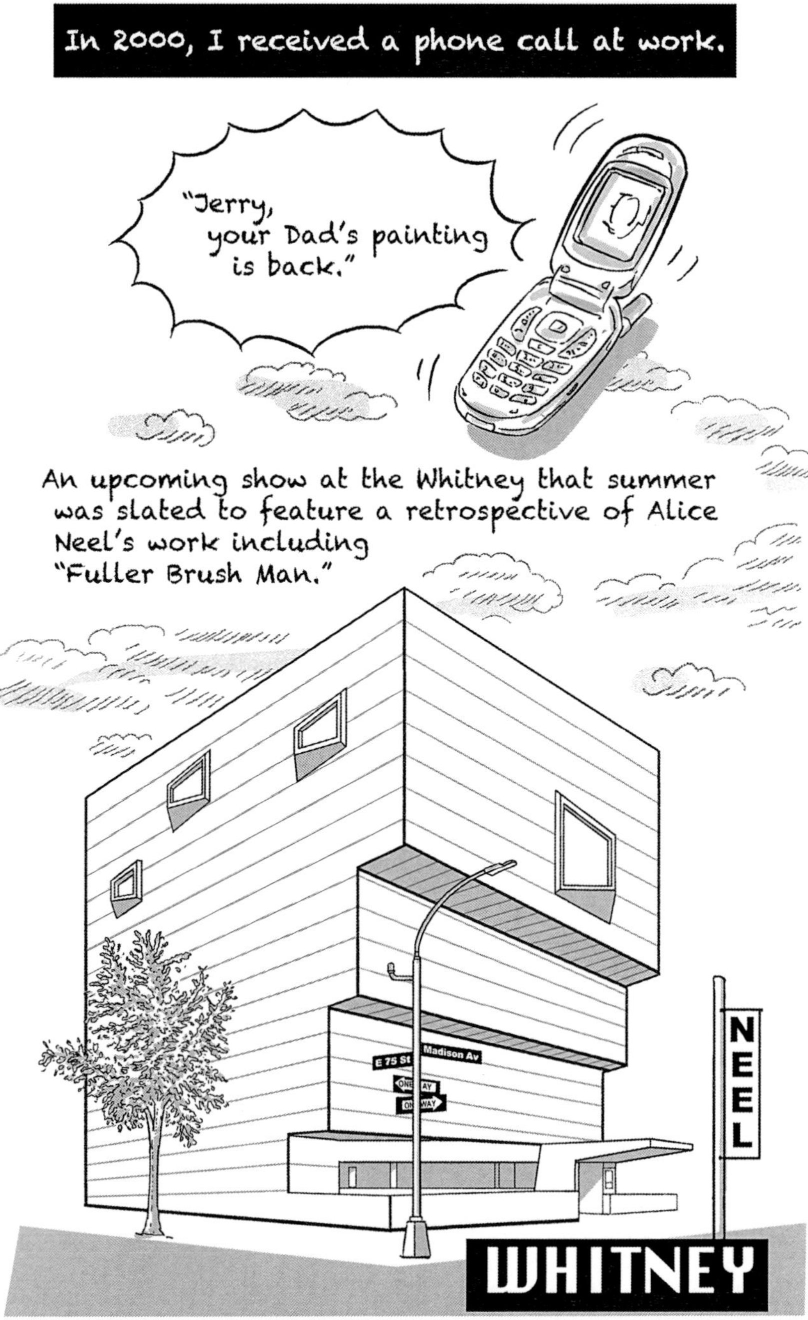
In 2000, I received a phone call at work.
"Jerry, your Dad's painting is back."
An upcoming show at the Whitney that summer was slated to feature a retrospective of Alice Neel's work including "Fuller Brush Man."
E 75 St
Madison Av
NEEL
WHITNEY

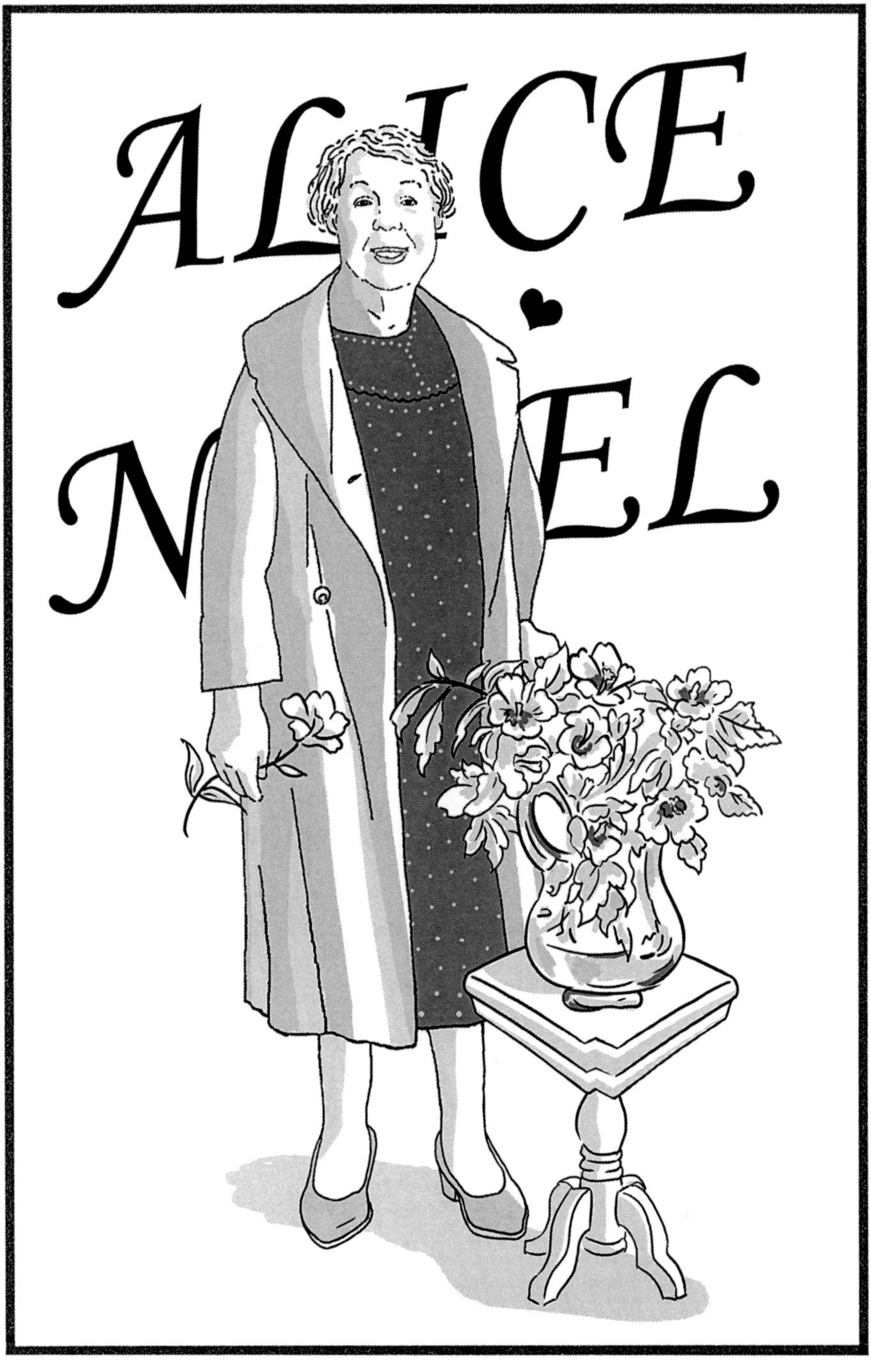
ALICE
N EL

Chapter 9:
The 2000 Whitney Centennial Show

WHITNEY

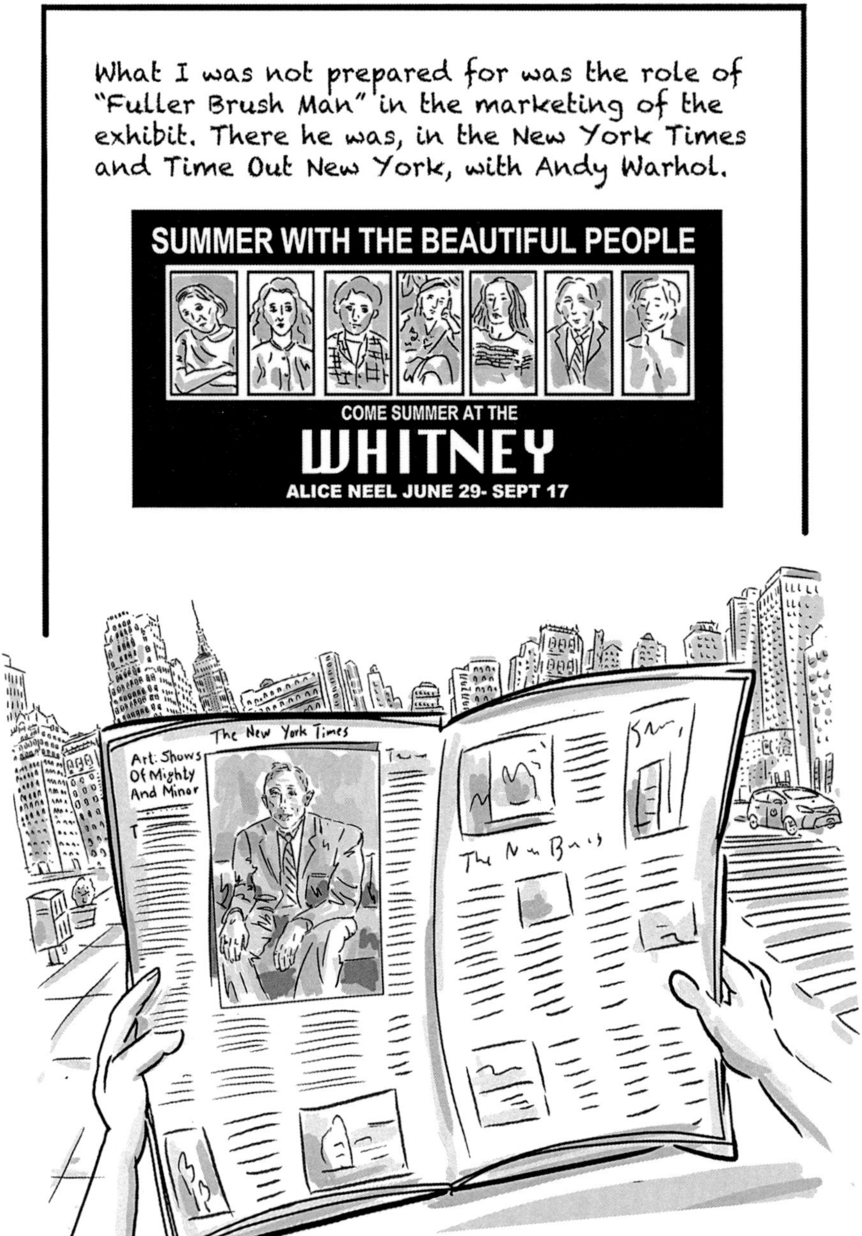
What I was not prepared for was the role of "Fuller Brush Man" in the marketing of the exhibit. There he was, in the New York Times and Time Out New York, with Andy Warhol.
SUMMER WITH THE BEAUTIFUL PEOPLE
COME SUMMER AT THE
WHITNEY
ALICE NEEL JUNE 29- SEPT 17
The New York Times
Art: Shows Of Mighty And Minor

But I think it was the mass transit advertising that really blew me away. Imagine walking down the street and being greeted by your Dad on the side of a bus.

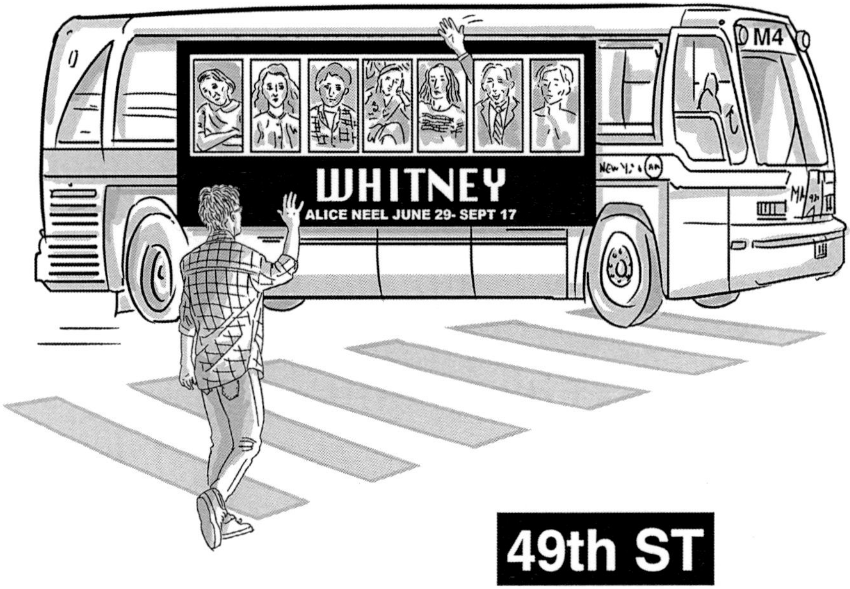
M4
WHITNEY
ALICE NEEL JUNE 29- SEPT 17
49th ST

Or walking down into the subway and seeing your Dad as you enter the 49th Street station. My brother was in town to see the show and considered swiping the poster from the subway station entrance, but we opted to contact the ad agency and ask for a copy.

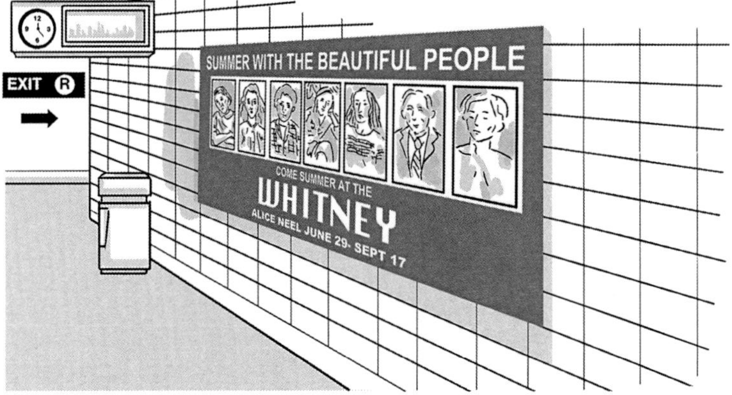
EXIT R
SUMMER WITH THE BEAUTIFUL PEOPLE
COME SUMMER AT THE
WHITNEY
ALICE NEEL JUNE 29- SEPT 17

I took my Aunt to see the painting at the Whitney. She looked at it and proudly said to any visitor that would listen, "That's my brother."

She was also interviewed by the local German-Jewish newspaper. My cousin came to see the picture and since initially viewing it in '84, had often imagined acquiring this now famous portrait. But it was in a private collection and no longer on the market.

10   KULTUR

Das Porträt von Alice Frasers Bruder Dewald Strauss

„Mein Bruder, der
Fuller Brush Man"

Ein Mann mit hellblauem Anzug schaut den Betrachter direkt an. In seiner Jackentasche stecken Pinsel. Ruhig, ehrlich und freundlich sieht dieser „Fuller Brush Man" auf dem Porträt der Malerin Alice Neel aus. Die Ausstellung im New Yorker Whitney Museum, durch die die Werke der Künstlerin einer breiten Öffentlichkeit bekannt werden, fand viel Beachtung. Alice Neels Lieblingsobjekte waren ausdrucksvolle Gesichter – von Familienmitgliedern, Freunden oder Menschen, die ihren Weg kreuzten. Einer dieser Menschen war Dewald Strauss, der „Fuller Brush Man" aus dem Whitney Museum und Alice Frasers Bruder.

Dewald Strauss wurde 1906 in Billigheit, in der Nähe von Heidelberg, geboren. Die Eltern hatten ein kleines Textilgeschäft. Nach der Schule zog er nach Regensburg, wo er bei einer Textilfirma arbeitete. Vor dort aus wurde er 1938 nach Dachau deportiert. Seine energische Mutter rettete ihm das Leben. Sie fuhr von Billigheit nach Regensburg zur Gestapo. Sie sagte den Polizisten: „Ich kann ohne meinen Sohn nicht leben." Dieser mutige Auftritt wurde Eindruck. Dewald Strauss wurde entlassen. Mit Unterstützung des Berliner Hilfsvereins (Aufbau berichtete darüber in der vergangenen Ausgabe) konnte er nach England reisen, bis Kitchener Camp in Sandwich und einen alten Freund ...

vereint in dem Haus in der 172nd in dem Alice Fraser noch heute wo ... Dewald Strauss lehnte noch ... scher Soldat wurde er in Anderm ... Rhein verwundet. Nach dem Krieg ... er seinen beiden Söhnen seinen G ...

In den ersten New Yorker Jahren lebte Dewald Strauss bei Textilfirmen. Anfang der 50er Jahre machte er ein Geschäft in der 195th Street, in dem er Fuller Brushes, Kosmetik und andere Produkte verkaufte. Es war eine sehr anstrengende Arbeit, die ihm dennoch Freude machte. Zu seinen Kunden zählte auch die Malerin Alice Neel, die in der Nachbarschaft lebte. „Sie war damals noch nicht berühmt. Niemand sprach über Alice Neel. Aber sie und mein Bruder haben sich gut verstanden", erklärt Alice Fraser. Eines Tages im Jahr 1965 brachte Dewald Strauss ein ...

52

One of the things that struck me about the show was how happy my Dad was compared to the other subjects, who appeared somber or depressed. Alice was known as a "collector of souls" and accurately captured my Dad's outlook on life- you never know what may happen next so here it is:

LIVE

LIFE

to the

Fullest

Chapter 10:
The Curator

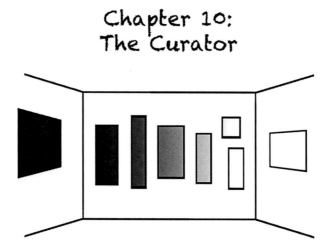

Curator, Alice Neel Exhibit
C/o The Whitney Museum
945 Madison Ave.
New York, NY

Dear Curator,

We were excited to be able to view the wonderful paintings of Alice Neel that have been selected for display at The Whitney. The subject of "The Fullerbrush Man" is our dearly departed father and brother, Dewald Strauss. The family would like to be kept abreast of the painting because of the importance it has played in demonstrating the extraordinary talent of Ms. Neel. It is nice to know that one can be remembered through the eyes of another in such graphic, and occasionally public fashion.

Mr. Strauss was born in Billigheim, Germany on July 4, 1906 and came to the United States in 1939 to escape Hitler's persecution of the Jewish people. After serving in World War II, he became a Fullerbrush dealer and ultimately gained Ms. Neel as a loyal customer. He married another German refugee, Ilse Reinach, and had two sons. He is also survived by his sister. He died on August 4, 1974 from heart disease. We think he would be proud to know that his portrait has been so admired and representative of Ms. Neel's body of work.

Please make every effort to get this letter to the current owners of the painting. We would hope that should it ever change hands, that we at least be made aware that it is being properly cared for to be admired by generations to come.

Sincerely,

Jerry Strauss (son)

Alice Neel's centennial exhibition was part of a larger road show, curated by Ann Temkin.
No one knew who he was but us, so I wrote to her and filled her in on my Dad's background.
I wanted Ann to know his name and that there was a larger story beyond the Fuller Brush Man who had survived Dachau.

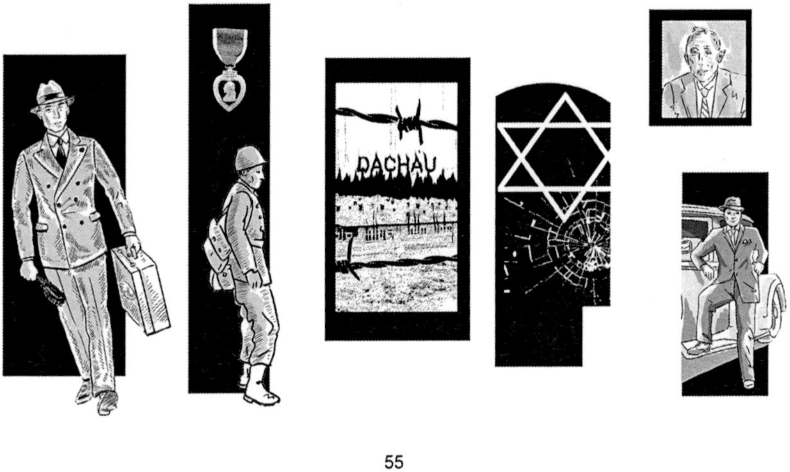
DACHAU

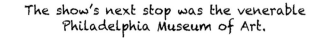

The show's next stop was the venerable
Philadelphia Museum of Art.

My boys and I went to see Grandpa's painting
at "Rocky's Museum."

Chapter 11:
The Man Has a Name!

Fuller Brush Man: *Mr. Dewald Strauss*

I was so happy when I saw his name on the label of the painting. I wrote down the label description on this brochure since I didn't have a camera with me. It was the first time my Dad's name had been recognized.

125th ANNIVERSARY YEAR

Exhibition Schedule 2001

FULLER BRUSH MAN -1965- OIL ON CANVAS

In celebration of its 125th Anniversary in 2001, the Museum presents a series of spectacular exhibitions showcasing the remarkable creative contributions of artists born or based in Philadelphia.

WHEN DEWALD STRAUSS, A DOOR-TO-DOOR SALESMAN FOR FULLER BRUSHES, STOPPED AT NEEL'S NYC APARTMENT SHE ASKED HIM TO POSE FOR A PORTRAIT. DURING THE COURSE OF THE SITTING, NEEL FOUND THAT STRAUSS WAS A CONCENTRATION CAMP SURVIVOR WHO, AFTER HIS ESCAPE HEROICALLY ENLISTED

Philadelphia Museum of Art

ONE HUNDRED AND TWENTY-FIFTH ANNIVERSARY 125

IN THE US ARMY AND RETURNED TO EUROPE TO FIGHT AGAINST THE NAZIS IN THE BATTLE OF THE BULGE,

Alice Neel

American, 1900-1984

Fuller Brush Man: *Mr. Dewald Strauss*, 1965
Oil on Canvas

When Dewald Strauss, a door-to-door salesman for Fuller Brushes, stopped at Neel's NYC apartment, she asked him to pose for a portrait. During the course of the sitting, Neel found that Strauss was a concentration camp survivor, who, after his escape, heroically enlisted in the US Army and returned to Europe to fight against the Nazis in the Battle of the Bulge.

The Fuller Brush Man finally had a name, my Dad, Mr. Dewald Strauss!

Alice Neel
American, 1900-1984

Fuller Brush Man: *Mr. Dewald Strauss*, 1965
Oil on Canvas

When Dewald Strauss, a door-to-door salesman for Fuller Brushes, stopped at Neel's NYC apartment, she asked him to pose for a portrait. During the course of the sitting, Neel found that Strauss was a concentration camp survivor, who, after his escape, heroically enlisted in the US Army and returned to Europe to fight against the Nazis in the Battle of the Bulge.

Acknowledgements

To Our Family and Friends
I am ever grateful to Lucia Yee-Lipitz for suggesting that we collaborate on this graphic novel adventure. We created this book with the love, input and inspiration of many of our family members and friends, and we send our heartfelt thanks to them all.

To Alice
Without Alice Neel, my family and I could have never experienced the incredible gift of "Fuller Brush Man." It has enabled us to remember Dad, not only through our fond memories and his unyielding spirit, but also through an indelible and beautiful visual experience, his amazing portrait. Alice Neel truly was a "collector of souls" and her passion to paint her friends, neighbors, and even a door-to-door salesman, has given us something we can cherish forever.

To the TEDx Producers
My sincere thanks to Limor Tomer, Christine Coulson, and Julie Burstein who expertly produced the TEDx and gave me the opportunity to publicly tell this story. My deep gratitude to Tom Campbell for leading the charge to present this riveting event for all to learn more about "The In-Between."

To the Curator
Thanks to Ann Temkin for recognizing my Dad as a unique individual and enabling me to "Give My Father Back His Name."

About the Author

Jerry Strauss has worked in Information Technology for decades but has always had a love for music, art and a good story. As a trumpet player, he has played in many a basement jam session and college gig. As a longtime employee of one of the world's greatest art museums, he had the chance to experience art on a daily basis. One day, at that museum, he had an opportunity to tell the story of his Dad, a Holocaust survivor, war hero, and the subject of a very famous portrait. That story has evolved into this book, which teaches us that there is a profound tale behind every picture.

About the Illustrator

Lucia Yee-Lipitz is an accomplished illustrator/designer who lives in New York. She loves books and all things nature.

For more on Lucia, go to http://www.luciayeelipitz.com.

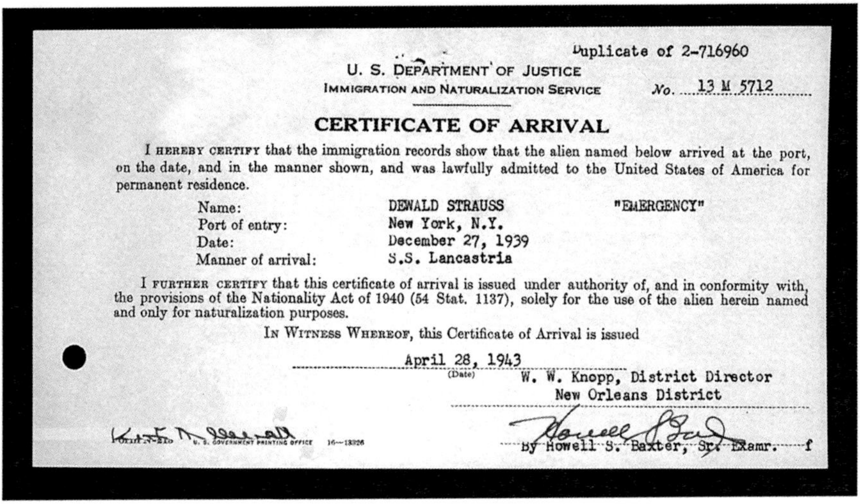

Duplicate of 2-716960

U. S. DEPARTMENT OF JUSTICE
IMMIGRATION AND NATURALIZATION SERVICE

No. 13 M 5712

CERTIFICATE OF ARRIVAL

I HEREBY CERTIFY that the immigration records show that the alien named below arrived at the port, on the date, and in the manner shown, and was lawfully admitted to the United States of America for permanent residence.

Name:	DEWALD STRAUSS	"EMERGENCY"
Port of entry:	New York, N.Y.	
Date:	December 27, 1939	
Manner of arrival:	S.S. Lancastria	

I FURTHER CERTIFY that this certificate of arrival is issued under authority of, and in conformity with, the provisions of the Nationality Act of 1940 (54 Stat. 1137), solely for the use of the alien herein named and only for naturalization purposes.

IN WITNESS WHEREOF, this Certificate of Arrival is issued

April 28, 1943
(Date)

W. W. Knopp, District Director
New Orleans District

By Howell S. Baxter, Sr. Examr. f

Form N-210 U. S. GOVERNMENT PRINTING OFFICE 16—13326

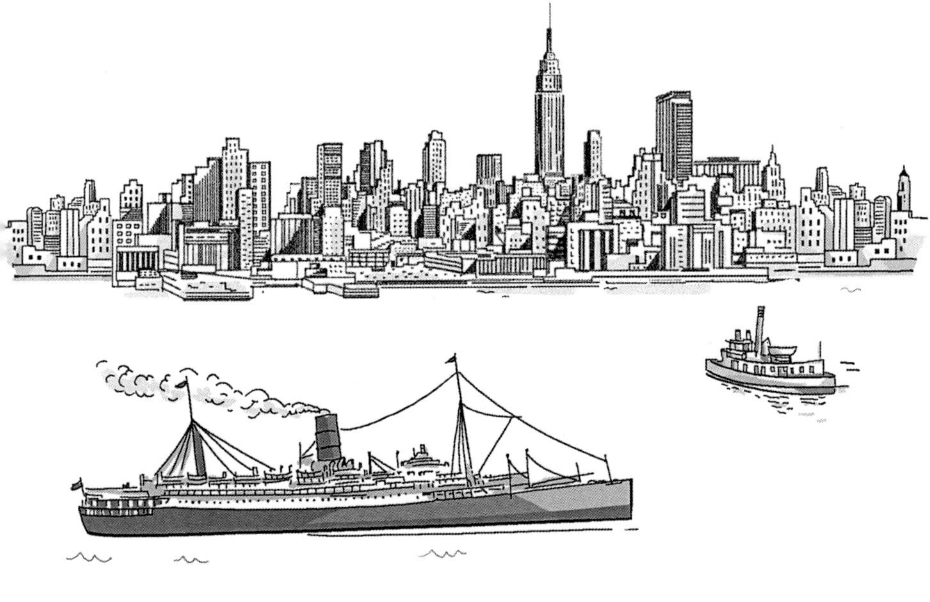

Vividly drawn and charmingly written. A true story about a Holocaust survivor, an artist, an iconic painting and the illuminating search that united them all.
Dr. Linda Burghardt, Scholar-in-Residence, Holocaust Memorial & Tolerance Center of Nassau County, N.Y.

In this wonderful recollection of a life well lived, Jerry Strauss has not only reclaimed his father's name but given us a memorable portrait (pun intended) of a former German-Jew who both suffered the torments of Dachau and shed blood for his adopted homeland to defeat Hitler's goal of destroying European Jewry. The Fuller Brush Man, Dewald Strauss, born on the fourth of July, is truly an American hero.
Abraham J. Peck, author of "The German-Jewish Legacy in America"

Jerry Strauss' moving memoir of his father, a Holocaust survivor, and his encounter with the incomparable Alice Neel, is a beautifully rendered tale. It is a great act of filial love that will lift your spirits and make you smile.
Fred Wasserman, Independent Curator

A door-to-door salesman meets a portrait artist who asks him to sit for her. The artist, Alice Neel, becomes famous years later as does her iconic painting "Fuller Brush Man." This is the story of the man behind the portrait, Dewald Strauss, his son's discovery of "Fuller Brush Man," and the struggle for his recognition as the true subject of the previously anonymous painting.

Giving My Father Back His Name

By Jerry Strauss with Illustrations by Lucia Yee-Lipitz
Cover Art and Design © 2020 by Lucia Yee-Lipitz

$17.95
ISBN 978-1-7923-5778-7
51795>

9 781792 357787